Lii

A Vision of Beauty

AE Reiff

Histericks 2023

For Annabellah, who shares Libby's initials, AER. and

for three hundred years of descendants from Jacob Reiff the Elder
(1698-1782) to Jacob Howard Reiff, 1908-1994) and their relations,
only son of an only son of folk born of Mennonites and Quakers of
the Palatine settlements in and around Germantown, Skippack,
Salford, Oley.

Acknowledgements

A search for beauty explores a family's memory of itself. Several generations preserved this culture. The family of **Kate Rosenberger**, an orphan who died in 1883, mother of Anna Elizabeth's father, **Howard R. Reiff**, was thought unknown until identified in a trail of names and initials on embroidered linens and show towels from 1772, confirmed against census records of that time. The letters of **Andrew S. Mack** (1836-1917), conciliatory bishop of the Mennonite church from 1875, Anna Bechtel Mack's uncle, appear here in English for the first time. He adopted Anna Elizabeth's mother Anna and her brother Will as young children for 2 years after their mother died. These 49 letters with the diary of his brother, Reverend **Peter Mack** of Hummelstown, (1842-1879), and the ledgers from 1875 to 1900 of **Henry Mack**, Anna Bechtel Mack's father (1854-1946), account their lives. Anna Bechtel Mack's doll creations, in combination with clippings of doll shows, identify her as a folk artist and linchpin of folk unity. Her life in this context contributes much to understanding what women of all families weave into being.

The greatest enabling of narrative here has been the four years of long distance telephone conversation with **Anna Elizabeth Reiff Young (1910-2005)** at the end of her life. These produced hundreds of pages of notes, like the *Times* crossword she did every night for decades, and absorbing to solve. She was a trained artist and antiquarian surrounded with a repository of furniture, pottery, art, quilts, embroideries, books and manuscripts of historical and religious backgrounds along with anecdotes and prejudices of those times. Archaic double day lilies from farms in Worcester a hundred years before grew in her gardens. As the New York buyer for a department store she added her own to the collection, visited twice a year from the far west to Philadelphia by myself, one or both sons, my wife, sometimes separately to foster their relationship, and by my brother's oldest son, Jorma. Sometimes we rented a van to tour with them the environs. On these visits we put up storm windows in fall and screens in spring. One summer I cemented the stoop. Her husband, Marvin Young, who she married at the age of 72, had an amazing collection of rare minerals and rocks in the basement to which my sons would repair after dinner to go over for hours. Fiercely independent, she lived alone in her nineties, coped successfully with lame feet, broken hips, replaced cataracts, transportation systems. Every day she demonstrated that there is a way to live without hope, but live anyway in hope for its own sake. Her long acerbic health evidences the best implication of aging. She relates the stories of her mother, **Anna Bechtel Mack Reiff (1880-1970),** which under the curatorship of this daughter occur in a context of ideas of the pietism of Johann Arndt, the mysteries of Jacob Boehm and the transcendentalism of quiet, unquiet ways of peace whose beauty lasts in the rigor, the wit and the boundaries they express.

Thanks to sons Aeyrie and Andrew for their good instincts in this effort and to Aeyrie for his company on frequent travels to Philadelphia. He turned the difficult into a joy. I am indebted to the invaluable work of Isaac R. Horst in translating the Andrew Mack letters of the Jacob B. Mensch collection and to the Mennonite Heritage Center for German copies of those letters, and to the Hummelstown Historical Society for research materials regarding Peter Mack. Two Mennonite congregations assisted, First Mennonite of Phoenix, a General Conference Mennonite church and the Conservative Mennonite Church of Paradise Valley, AZ who generously loaned me their copy of *Martyr's Mirror* or *The Bloody Theater.* Harry E. Reiff, the genealogist and organic chemist, has been a valued ally and friend. His cogent insights brought to my attention unknown details with the important luxury of conversing with someone expert in such matters. Relatives on every side have contributed knowingly and unknowingly. To all of them I owe my thanks and most of all to my wife for her constant love and support. Several proofs of this work exist, *A Red Portfolio: The Life of a Pennsylvania Dutch Radical* (2004), *Portrait of a Lady* (October 2004), *A History of the Last Days* (November 2004) and *The Way into the Flowering Heart* (18 Sept 2005). This last was to have been the version published here until rereading *A Red Portfolio* required interlineating the whole. A raisonné of Libby's work appears at Artist Anna Elizabeth Reiff Young 1910-2005 Life at 90 and A Study of Interiors.

Contents

Folk Life Weaving 157

Authority of the Living, Natural heir, Weaving Begins at the
Bottom, Commercials, Ignorance, Boehme, Folk Artist, Curator
Challenge to History, Grandma, Denial of History, Alan Watts,
Stretching the Original, Retelling, Folk Take, Refinishing the
Classics, Taking Down Buddha, Taking Down the Tree, Facts as
Artifacts, Folk ID.

A Day in the Life 177

The Humor of Defect, Abraham: A Day in the Life, Acme,
Cartilage, Ophelia, Balaam, Matzo, McHusband & McWife, Many
Subjects, Dogged, Starlings, Men, Hair with Wings, Icons,
Boundary, Mad at God, CEO, Time's Up, Make Believe Life,
Defects of Defects, Attic & Basement.

Farewell Sorrow 203

End of an Era, 9/9, 9/15, 9/21, 9/22, 9/27,9/29, 9/30, 6/10, 6/19,
6/20, 6/27, 6/28. Blackbird Green Light, 11/1, 11/13, 11/24, 11/30,
12/7, 12/9, 12/15. Don't Drive At Night, 4/6/2005, 4/20.

Watercolors in the Attic

The search for beauty starts in an attic among watercolors. That's where her great grandfather's signature celebrating his ownership of a copy of *Die Wandelnde Seele* in 1835 was, and the name "Maria Lapin" stitched in citron on a linen sheet, 1772, and the embroidery of her father's grandmother, Margaret Gehman, of a white tulip blooming from a heart, 1851. By the time her grandfather Henry Mack recorded his love for "my darling Lizzie," in his Ledger of the 1870's, the quest had momentum. Henry partly escaped the peasant destiny remembered by his daughter Annie when he came in from the fields at noon sometimes too exhausted to eat, he took only a glass of warm water for food. Annie, born 1880, prepared to leave the farm long before her actual departure in 1901.

How She Got Her Mind

Our subject, Anna Elizabeth, made a complete effort with those generations toward an intellectual life. She was the first artist and intellectual but the last surviving family Dutchman. She says, "I don't know where I got my mind," as if she had contracted for a buggy but got an airplane instead. In this perception of a first class mind we look among the artifacts of that Pennsylvania Dutch nurture that surrounded her with a host of domestic particulars in her mother's gardens full of tiger lilies, borders of tulips and herbs, dozens of pots of African violets on every window sill, extraordinary pies, cakes, coffees and roasts, doughnuts made whole by the kitchen artist, Gaudy Dutch plates and cups, old when her mother's grandmother had them, hymns she sang at multiple church services, the handmade Berks county country chest with its chamfered drawers, walnut wood and heavy boards, her grandfather's blanket chest with its porcelain knobs kept in the attic next to old trunks with her father's initials and his father's, filled with the show towels and double-stitched woolen car blankets, bedspreads and linens alongside shipping boxes of chocolate from her father's warehouse: Walter Baker & Co. Ltd., Premium No. 1 Chocolate, and large metal containers of sugar from the Franklin Sugar Refining Co., Philadelphia. Artifacts, vases, Stangl ceramics, hymns at countless church services as a girl, Mennonite Sunday School at 9:30, services at 11, Tioga Presbyterian Sunday School at 2:30 where her teacher was Jesse Isabel Barclough, wife of the Scotsman, Henry Barclough, composer of "Out of the Ivory Palaces," then back to the Mennonite Christian Endeavor at 7 PM followed by the evening service hymn sing at 8, the background and sometimes the foreground of her mind were so filled with these folk images it was an easy thing to translate into being a New York buyer of gifts for her department store, which she did for 35 years. The hint from household artifacts and gardens interpreted with hymns as mutual quotations about flowers, roses, lilies, and morning-stars expressed in jewelry, pottery, and linens, was a "use of natural events and objects to describe spiritual conditions" (Stoudt, 100).

Four Levels

That Media house had four levels, attic to basement. The attic was an unfinished A with a floor and windows at both ends, pervasive with the smells of sycamore, rock wool, bare beams and wood. My venture in the discovery of her art begins there where I used to stare from my cot on overnight visits in the half light of morning at the oranges and apples shadowed in a green bowl on a table piled high and dark on the top of old wardrobes and feel reflections play off the canvas.

I wanted to know, whose art is it? Why is it in the attic? Then later, where did it go? No answers were given. Implications broadened. Denials flamed. The child must have been bothersome, but was getting warm as a young man when she denied there had ever been any paintings at all. What she should have said was, with a superior sniff, "Oils! Dear boy, I'm a watercolorist," meaning a lyricist, a soloist.

Full sheets of these watercolors, with her notebooks, were found in the cleaning and inventory of that attic. She studied art for four years at Moore College of Art & Design, graduated, and painted formally for four years. I found thirteen full sheets of watercolor interiors sometimes architectured like a Rilke sonnet, colors fresh. They had been rolled up in the attic. A few had water stains from the leaking roof. The best were immaculate when cleaned. I photographically reproduced and digitally enlarged the details. The carvings of wood blocks, meticulously graphed interiors with measurements to the eighth inch, along with nine shades of brown alone are tested in a notebook for her watercolor of the furniture of "Pennsylvania Room." Pennsylvania Dutch designs are shadowed above and below the wallpaper behind the tables and among the chair rungs. The full sheets of heavy paper were stretched onto boards, the perimeter glued and the whole wet. When finally executed the paper was cut free. I also have the boards.

There is affection for furniture in her work, as though images were gardens, a metaphor of her life, an interior landscape. As the large lengthwise cushion of "Sheraton Settee" reflects sunlight, it seats at least six across, the long upholstered panel alternates vertical pale yellow stripes with light green shown to be worn where the backs of people rested. A shading of pale yellows shows the cushion is curved, washing pale to a more constant yellow at the top and from the middle up and down the stripes. An outline of four spindled legs equidistant from each other frames the whole, The metaphor of wear, color, time, age contained by the brown edges suggests a gold green alchemy like sun on grass.

"Pennsylvania Room - Philadelphia Museum," presents a trestle table with a pitcher, vase and old book held by metal clasps,

much like the *Wahren Christenthum* in her attic inscribed with the name of her great grandfather, Abraham Bechtel. Above the table is an image of a woman in a bonnet, to the right a spindle-backed wooden chair below a country cupboard, to the left another wooden chair. Folk designs embroidered on the wall paper, baskets

of flowers, borders, part of a barn, a rooster as the designs continue under the table and chairs and interweave with the shadows. Her sketchbook shows how each detail was prepared, measured, identified: front stretcher, its dimensions, side stretcher, its dimensions, the chair, positive and negative space identified, measured. Different versions of wallpaper exist, but the one chosen, designed on hand drawn graph paper, has each detail magnified before finished execution.

I was invited by those visits in the attic to enter the participation mystique of the natural that preoccupies *Pennsylvania German Folk Art,* this Congregation of the Truly Inspired, the *Inspirationsgemeinde* (Max Goebel). Participation is as important as the meaning in the garden within and without. In bringing the garden into the house in furniture, flower, quilt, chest, fireplace and into the heart in hymnals of devotional poetry, two songs blend into one.

Desire for the Beautiful

I argue from the image of the sun in the sky implicit in the settee's cushion, the watercolor of green and gold that bursts in my mind, where is the mature body of this work? In the last four years of her life she would take up my speculations. I asked why she didn't at least paint frakturs. "Too tired," she said, "from the long days." Did she remember her great, great maternal grandfather's name signed in that book in her attic, along with his son, and her maternal grandmother of a long line of Mennonite ministers?

Her mother's family was Mennonite from the founding of Pennsylvania, her father's the same. Surrounded by the artifacts of a dozen lives kept perfectly can be no accident, but there was no intellectual transmission until the last by intuitive discovery. Five embroidered linens of the deceased Catherine G. Rosenberger, mother of Howard R., unraveled the mysteries like the Bechtel books that slept in the attic did theirs. In a large trunk, linens and blankets had been brought out for viewing maybe every twenty years. The linens, show towels, one embroidered sheet, and one sampler constitute remains as personal as signed books. The show towels are signed and dated in every case like the books with documentation that opens a door into those minds.

Realism

"Do you deny that what I saw in my mind all the years from childhood was these paintings?" I'd be afraid of the denial, except my memory is unshakeable, as detailed as the paintings exhibited on the walls at Van Gogh's viewing. Is she ignorant of her influence, this long aged figure of Beatrice? To prove it to her I wrote this work, to prove to her it matters if another feels the same longing she did. The canvases are stretched in the negative space of the road not taken. I style her with the late nineteenth century French poet, Arthur

Rimbaud (1854-1891) celebrated for renouncing his greatness at 19 to never write another word, so that the work she never did, accepting that it was never done, makes her a Pennsylvania Dutch Rimbaud who accomplished a dissolution by retailing.

The glory of this "realism" boasts tiger stripes of beauty and austerity. "Not good enough for fine art," she replies with self-effacement when I ask, "not a genius." She sacrificed to work, provide a home, protect her mother, did not become an artist in the Pennsylvania Dutch manner or any other. It's as if she lived on the farm. She invented as many ways to doubt her work as her own beauty: upbringing, gender, poverty, religion, for beauty might not recognized among folk if they thought it consumed by truth. Pietists, Mennonites sought truth and God for their own sake, but where was beauty hid if it might be associated with pleasure? So the quest for beauty contains contradiction, Beethoven running down stairs to finish a chord, high passion and dudgeon. Borges, god of the fabulists, called a priest at the end of his life, buried near Calvin in Geneva. It will be said an aberration, but it was Maria; that he didn't mean it, that old age turns men weak, but the true weakness is youth, like Rimbaud's madness, drugs and guns and preaching about prophets when he was not one, for to be a prophet means more than erratic speech. At the end of his life Rimbaud called on God, had a priest and came to equipoise. They must exhaust themselves first. George Herbert commanded his brother to burn his poems. Michelangelo burned his drawings. Donne circulated only hand written copies. Dickinson hid in her room. Hopkins burned all his early work and Blake, taking the gouge to Plate 3 of *Jerusalem* effaced every suggestion of affection for and approbation from the reader, which seriously touches my friend and namesake Anna Elizabeth Reiff Young, who like all these persons was in mortal conflict with the proviso that one should not reveal. As Wittgenstein said, *what can be said at all can be said clearly; and whereof one cannot speak thereof one must be silent, especially since it will only*

be understood by those who already have the thought. In the self
submerged endemic from Shakespeare to Eliot the great freedom is
freedom from oneself. Who survives their immolation by doing the
work and burning it or burning it by not doing it? Realism or genius!
Such lengths restore beauty in our memories, dig up manuscripts
from Rossetti's grave, thankfully save one surviving colored copy of
Jerusalem. Of the work of her maturity there is no Libby except
what is written here.

A Red Portfolio

She asked if I had seen a red portfolio in the attic that contained all the free work she had done since, as watercolors should be done, she said, freehand, for the joy of living. This gambit removes her entirely from the world of the mundane, since the action it implies puts her in the company of _Le poète assassiné_ of compulsion, the follies that all the best of those we most love seem to practice. She casts the nerve and pain with aplomb. She shredded the red portfolio in a fury of rejection at her husband, tore them up in his face.

Had I seen these in a large red portfolio in the attic?

No, there was no sign of them.

"I guess I threw them away."

This is quite a prank, laughable not only because she is not guessing and knows very well what happened, but because she did not just throw them away.

She ripped them up before his eyes.

The story comes out. In the midst of some sort of discussion or other, and uncharacteristically wanting to reveal herself further, she had shown them to husband Marvin, another Dutchman of the generations who had such fierce ideas about art that he then and there declared they weren't art! So equally then and there, in high dudgeon, she destroyed them in front of his eyes in a passionate fury. It's nice to compare this with the time the rejected Blake furiously gouged every word with a chisel from the copper plates of _Jerusalem_ that suggested his "love," or "friendship" for the reader, "all traces of personal intimacy and spiritual communion."

Destroying the red portfolio is an *auto-da-fé* in the tradition of the burning of German devotional books continued by Peter Miller and Conrad Weiser in 1732. Miller, who served a term as pastor of the Reiff Church of Skippack 1730-31, the first Reformed church in Philadelphia, was one of the great linguists of the American colonies who translated the *Martyrs' Mirror* from the original Dutch to German. He and Conrad Weiser, interpreter and diplomat of native nations, immolated the Heidelberg Catechism just to prove they were not Lutherans, but true Sabbatarians, not the last immolation of that century according to the critic Julius Friedrich Sachse (I, 245). But the red portfolio wasn't even the first such immolation of her own family. Before she had ever graduated art school her brother, J. Howard, had profoundly destroyed their errant grandfather's estate papers. Later accounts that he just didn't pick them up differed from the earlier report of their burning. Of course the child hearer is not supposed to remember such things. Libby's mother Anna destroyed every letter she got after she had read it (but not the post cards!), not from anger, but with the belief that once read the letter was worthless! Why did she save all the post cards? Flurries of cold reconciliation swirl about. That is why antiquarian Jacob Mensch's saving of the 49 letters of Andrew Mack is such a rarity and exception. Libby pulls the aplomb of decades of destruction around her, says, "you'll get over it," as if she did.

I don't. I piece the shreds together, array the clues of her attic, basement, china cabinet, chests. If this rejection of the body of books, papers, or whatever oeuvre is a paradigm, it's not art, letters, estate papers or devotions that offend, it is a habit of expression. When she had retired to her new home in the hospital towers at $300 a day, a desk drawer of meticulous dailies of the 70's and 80's was found that yielded no personal comments or observations of any kind. Asked what she wanted to do with them, she replied, "I'll get my lawyer to burn them." She declares she has old records of her trip to Greece. Shall she send them to me or "tear them up?" This is not limited. My wife's grandmother after moving to Texas in 1920 burned all the letters she got from her sisters in Sweden. Her recipe book was handed down though, except that her daughter glued recipes cut from magazines over the original handwritten ones in Swedish.

Hearing all this, but not really in an attempt to get even, I sent some writing to husband Marvin, who liked to write, with the advice that it should be drunk with a bucket of sea water. *Vulcan* revered it (Pancake Syntazz (66-71) and *Eyeshot* thought it *wayward* with symbolic acts. I also gave Libby an acrylic, returned after her death, where earth and sky wrote yellow cursives of swirls of blue, white and brown, a language not reduced to formula, to remind her, like the brushstroke swirls of her great grandfather's signature, that the outdoors can come in. Even though the road is not taken the road is taken.

So the Red Portfolio was gone, but left behind conundrums that didn't fit the world of art school and watercolor socials but went nicely with annihilation. It went with the sardonic, critical view of the foibles and follies of life. It went so well it fueled four years of riposte by phone, hours by the week, and thorns for the crucified when she had no fame and hardly any visitors, but survived anyway on the slender pickings of teasing calls and packages of oranges and apples appearing mysteriously on the porch. She never got it that these were sent to her in homage of her still life oils, that is, returned in fruit. She only became famous when she was able to declare herself terminal and was admitted into the niceties of permanent care. Then governed, wit made nice. Her walls held photographs and paintings of which she might consider herself part muse. Her nightstand held copies of bound versions of this work celebrating herself. If I will assume what she assumed, there is a long while yet to drive back the shadows that burn, torched by light. In the end the great Peter Miller of Ephrata, of the *Chronicon Ephratense* exploring life in the Ephrata community, retired to live out his years quietly on a farm in Skippack. Do we get ever over the destiny generations tried so hard to attain?

Art School

Considering all this she is asked, "why did you go to art school? "I didn't want to be a teacher."

Why did you go to art school?

"Well I wanted to be a doctor but that didn't go over at home." The evasion rings true, for the earthen despises entitlement so much that after she finished art school and painted murals for cash, floral scenes on walls for rich ladies such as Mrs. Sheldeker on Oak Lane, when the rich insisted on having her driven home by chauffeur, for this patronizing attitude she terminated the position. What she lacked wasn't talent or money. It was hubris. She was a reverse genius who believed the opposite so strongly that it didn't matter what others did.

A Fragrant Husband

The irony is that in the first part of the 18th century her paternal families weren't immediately Mennonites or poor farmers. They had farms and were educated professionals and founded, amid controversy the first Reformed church in Pennsylvania while others were leaders among the New Born of Oley. As political and social leaders they were already everything that Anna eight generations later wanted to be. Before Anna ever sought to escape the accent, the farm and country ignorance, these forebearers spoke multiple languages, including English and held public office. Anna Mack must have sensed a deep fragrance of the life she wanted in her husband Howard R. Reiff's background.

That first new world progenitor, Hans George Reiff, settled his family in Salford at least by 1717 (Strassburger, 414). Although no Mennonite, he signed his name "with a firm hand" (Heckler) as witness to the Mennonite Trust agreement of 1725 that allocated land for a burial ground and school. Maybe he even put this agreement into English. The terms of his will show him to be wise and implicitly educated. Genealogists consider his wife, Anna, famously buried in the Mennonite burial ground in 1753 to a eulogy of Muhlenberg, to have been the daughter of Dutch Reformed church minion.

Hans son, Jacob the Elder, "was entrusted by the Colonial government as agent to go around among the settlers to collect partial payments on their lands in 1723. He must have been here some time before, well acquainted, and in the confidence of the leading men" (Dotterer quoted in Heckler, 31). This Jacob was Philadelphia County assessor in 1741, deputy for the probate of wills for Philadelphia County, 1743 to 1748. Heckler in his *Historical Sketches* (1886) says he was "the most prominent man in the early history of Salford" and among the four most "reasonably well educated" men of the area who were classically trained, "a man of great force of character."

The next generation's oldest son, again a Jacob, was the first elected member of the Pennsylvania General Assembly from Montgomery County (1786-89). He voted for the Convention to adopt the Constitution of the United States. He was one of several founders of the Wentz Reformed Church which continued the Skippack Reformed Church, the first Reformed Church in Pennsylvania, begun by his father and grandfather. The second son,

George (1740-1808), from whom Libby descends, became a Mennonite, married Elizabeth Hendricks, daughter of Leonard Hendricks, son of the immigrant Lawrence Hendricks, part of the so-called Krefeld group who settled Germantown in 1683 whose progenitor signed the anti-slavery tract in 1688.

George and Jacob's cousins were sons of the Conrad Reiff who ended up in possession through marriage of the estates of the founders of the New Born of Oley, Matthius Bauman and Philip Kuhlwein. These cousins, Daniel and Phillip Reiff, were listed as officers in the Berks Co. Militia during the Revolution. All of these wives were likewise educated, wrote and spoke English, were mentioned honorably in contemporary affairs many of which activities might fall under later Mennonite prohibition, but how many generations does it take to get assurance for the immigrant mind? Compelled to raise the questions here just because the puzzle is in front of my eyes I do it because from the earliest age she was the image of beauty to my mind.

When she first declared herself terminal with cancer an early draft of this was rushed out for her to read, a thousand disorganized details.

"People are going to ask me whether you read this, but it's very chaotic, the Mennonites, for instance crop up everywhere. What do I tell them?"

"That's the way it is with me, the Mennonites are always following me around mentally. I'm still a Mennonite in some way or other."

Works Cited

William Blake. *Jerusalem.* Edited by Morton D. Paley. Princeton: William Blake Trust. 1998.

James Y. Heckler. *The History of Harleysville and Lower Salford Township*. 1886. Bedminster, PA: Adams Apple Press, 1993.

Sachse, Julius Friedrich. *The German Sectarians of Pennsylvania*. Philadelphia, 1899. NY: AMS Press, 1971,

Strassburger, Ralph Beaver. *The Strassburger Family and Allied Families of Pennsylvania*. Privately Printed: Gwynedd Valley, Pa. 1922, 414.

John Joseph Stoudt. *Pennsylvania German Folk Art*. Allentown, PA: Schlechter's, 1966.

J. C. Wenger. *History of the Mennonites of the Franconia Conference*. Telford, PA: Franconia Mennonite Historical Society, 1937. Republished by Mennonite Publishing House. Scottdale, PA, 1985.

Are You Only a Physical Being?

Walking Tour

I meditated upon her life for decades. She said she tried very hard to leave it in God's hands, but my memory returns to the attention she lavished on my brother and I from the earliest age. As a coup de grace at 21 she gave me her insider's walking tour of New York City. But the weekly conversations I had with her by phone those last years were a walking tour through her mind, down to the three inch Christmas tree she had on her table one year.

I could call it her post Rimbaud period except almost everything was post Rimbaud. It's not that I believe the work, the art, the woodcuts, the watercolors weren't done, but they did not survive. Death notices of family members, behests and bequests survived. I still don't know where she hid the rest that I couldn't find. I found so much, but it always felt incomplete.

Maybe these notes compensate, taken with the same idea I had of the last decade of the 20th century, to get the best I could find of literature before the millennium's end. When the 20th century died I ceased collecting it. Now she is gone I harvest the notes, but there is always more. There were metaphor-laden multiple subtexts to her thinking. Her mind is like her house, her literal home in Media of four stories, with her whole sense of family, the culture of which she is a part and her own mortal being.

Are You Only A Physical Being?

I call her today, my 62nd birthday because her courage inspires me.

So right away she asks me "are you only a physical being?"

What kind of a question is that on your birthday? I can't say yes. It's been a struggle to be a physical being.

If it weren't for my wife I might not be a physical being. I don't tell her that after I shouldered the burden of her estate, which was more than physical, prepared it, packed it and drove it across an entire country, that I had constant lightning flashes in my eyes and one night extreme dizziness that lasted two months till the brain rewired itself. Physical being has impediments, blood scans, pulse rates and ACL's. I had to wear a heart monitor because my resting pulse was 40, but I had consciously wanted it low all these years. As they are now considering a pacemaker I want it higher. Am I only a physical being? Do I still want to grasp the universe and bring it to earth? I can't tell her that. At the club where I train there are daily reminders of physical being. How do these people get so misshapen? But the outward is not as bad as its complement. How do they get so misshapen within?

Be Grateful for the Way You Are

This is her lead in to tell me of her week where she has three times taken public transit to appointments for eye, tooth and foot care.

On the first ride she was picked up by a very old black man as driver who with great authority said to her, "I hope you're grateful to God for being the way you are," meaning, able to live alone and navigate the transit system by herself at 94. She was impressed. He spoke to her with the authority of a priest. I have met this man in other places. He is an angel. They perused the matter further.

The follow-up, on the second trip, to the dentist, was with another slightly less old black driver, who had her age on the pickup form. He said the same words, as if the whole thing were scripted, "I hope you're grateful for being able to do what you do at your age." You don't need to see them to benefit from them or believe in them for that matter. I don't tell her he was an angel. Let her savor the moment. Two different drivers saying the same thing on two different trips gets her to thinking. Her thinking is this:

Why Am I Alive?

"My father died at 47, my mother at ninety, my sister at 49 and my brother at 85. God must have a reason for me to still be here." It's funny to believe in the reason but not know what it is. Again I am silent but I am filled with gratitude that she is being taken care of.

She would not believe that the reason of her being here is as my consolation, that she is a gift to me from the Lady Philosophy.

I enter the argument with only the bland comment that she has always lived with ideas and aesthetics and being way too austere for the world to accept, plus the obvious spiritual connotations of her thinking, may have to accept, but grudgingly the health and long life in her. Not to speak of the very independent nature which makes her do everything for herself. She says she was 72 before she first felt tired. That's when she got married the first time. That's what marriage will do to you.

Apropos of this she's going to reread Paul Tournier's *The Seasons of Life*.
He says that of the four seasons, winter is the one where **you don't do, you just be** and that… *At the heart of personality is the need to*

feel a sense of being lovable without having to qualify for that
acceptance.

Don't do, just be, as in the long day. Why she's almost the
age of Abraham.
Maimonides says being green and supple in old age means
bearing children. I tell her I wish her the generic not the specific.

The Long Day

What time is it in her long day? She has a standing joke, and
it is a rule, she will receive not guests before 10 AM. It takes a long
time no matter where you live to dress and get into support stockings
alone. Her ankles have largely failed after walking literally
everywhere all her life and there is a circulation problem. Husband
Marvin's pills used to take an hour all by themselves, but she jokes
that when the old body shuts down the sweat glands don't work so
well and you can save time on baths, just the thing any twelve year
old boy is after. And you have less laundry!

On the flip side you will always be laughing at the
absurdities of life, teeth, glasses and lists, but only when you live
alone do you talk to yourself, which she confesses to. When you go
terminal, go hospice, go life care, there are way too many people
watching to laugh or talk, so you need to behave. Even turning
ninety, breaking her hip didn't tie her down, so she got the cataract
out but then the gall bladder broke.

"I make lists, plenty of them, because I have lots of old
paper, even if it is yellowing around the edges. Then I tear them up.
But I have a hard time throwing away old paper so I make new lists."

The yellowing edges of the image, the old paper stored in drawers, the disposable lists like the bygone year have plenty still to write on to pass time and life in The Day.

Here is a hat hard enough to wear to keep from banging against the passions of happy hour, those disasters of inattention, but not exclusive to alcohol you know, somebody who's not willing to temporize in order to get along, someone with her short term memory intact.

Folk authorities will always be missed most in times of crisis, this latest, the sinking of New Orleans leaves no one left to appeal to in confidence with the assurance that whatever they say will be comforting. I could always in his later years confide in my father and in her.

What Is the Divine Purpose?

She doesn't understand why her left leg betrayed her when she fell. I too had that feeling when I backed out of my driveway into the path of an oncoming car and was creamed. Was it the eyes, the brain, the attention span failed? The questions go on and on. We must try to answer them honestly.

Amish Mennonites have a take on this. This guy on the way to Nebraska at Christmas ran out of gas twice, going and coming on the same trip. Invoking divine purpose, he said it must have been because he was supposed to talk to tow truck drivers and cops. He's serious!

Does it help you to understand such speech if you know his father is a Mennonite Elk hunter?

A three shell man!

Anyway, she concludes that her left leg had a heavier burden on it since the right leg had already worn out its tendons, which made her limp. Simply, she turned around too quickly, lost her balance. The word arthritis occurred in this, but I have the same problem with arthritis that she does with Abraham. Myth. I told her I don't believe in it. She can't feel anything in two toes. Our pain is mutual. It holds us hostage to life, but we don't think that it has meaning for anyone else do we? My pain is for me! And what do I learn? To activate the senses? But not like my dog just now putting up her nose in the air and howling at the crane that is cleaning out the canal. To live noble lives we have to own our pain, not pretend it's for someone else's good. Either that or we may take the high road John Arndt sets out below, that our purgation is our perfection and we should only be concerned if things are going well.

I love it when the deniers of pain talk about Job. Then all kinds of e-mail tales and fine stories of rescue are told, but never personal. Nobody there got themselves rescued. Just like in the previous era none of them were stoned either. They just heard about it. She lived it. What a setup.

I tell her how the Mennonite Sunday School came up with a story about pain from *Guideposts*, as an exemplary piety. A father was watching his son and another boy drown. The father believed he could only save one of them, so he reasoned that because the other boy was "unsaved" and his son would "go to heaven," he should save the other boy. The respondent asked the narrator what happened to the saved boy. The man pointed to the pulpit. "He's the pastor."

I get angry at nonsense like this, say things I shouldn't, like, "you'll never meet a pastor like that," (they all drowned). The proffered choice is a false dilemma, the glorification of pastors at any cost. "Whose PR department wrote that?" What a good man he was, to condemn his own son. Why it sounds just like the Bible. Did the guy think he was Abraham. "Do you ever stop to question your assumptions?"

That was the second point. While this dude was sacrificing his son, what was that boy thinking, my own father won't save me? That's what Kierkegaard said in *Fear and Trembling*. What was Isaac thinking while his father raised the knife over his head? Kierkegaard's solution, Abraham acted as if he were mad in order to save his son's faith. For how could Isaac trust in a God who ordered his death? I'm telling all this to her admittedly because she is sensitive about her Abraham, but she says,

"I never understood Kierkegaard."

So I gave her a blast about the background narrative of the Hebrew text that left such detail out just for that purpose, so you might participate, the opposite of the Greek where all that foreground description occurs. In the Greek, Isaac would be pictured in his agony, Abraham and Sarah would have been heard arguing, "where did you say you were going again dear and why?"

But her stepson Bruce is in for it too. He came home from brain surgery at Temple Hospital after only 4 days. His old tumor of the esophagus had metastasized. They got it all....

So yes, I got nailed by a pregnant immigrant lady in a red car who drove off. What is that a symbol of? I chased her dragging my bumper, but the referent was too heavy.

Seizing any pretext I teased my wife about it, "how are you going to maintain the notion that I'm invincible? "

But she has learned this from breaking her hip. The two are similar, one minute you take a step, the next you are down. How did I get here?

"The Lord was telling me that my plans were not his plans."

"Did you find our what His plans were?"

"Not yet."

Ask Abraham. The Lord will affront the raging realism.

"Neither height nor depth, nor angels or powers, things past or to come, not any created thing is able to separate you from my love."

I clipped the hedge surrounding the drive, but let slip that Mennonites for all of that seem genuine.

She will not be coddled, mumbles, "being genuine is not limited to the lower middle class."

Their Last Drive

But now Media is battening down for the coming hurricane and those terrorist preparations are useful too, the batteries with long life, the water. Her husband Marvin always looked prepared, like he was ready for rain or sun, as odd a duck as he was. He wore pitch black heavy sunglasses, a tam o'shanter and sweaters all the time. He drove right up to the end, was 94 himself. You did well to see them coming.

But this week she was driven up to Coopersburg with Marvin's ashes to put them in the grave next to his first wife, Stella. They actually dug up the grave and put the box in. We should stop here and think, do I want this to happen to me?

Yes women do all the dirty work. They were at the tomb of the Lord. Anna was in scraping old Jacob off the floor. She is digging up Stella's grave so Marvin can wake up next to her at the resurrection. I don't think love is a duty and I don't think she does either. Love is a pain. So she says to me, "it was a nice diversion". A painless drive, a comfortable car, and thou. She has plans to be buried across town in North Philadelphia with her mother, father and sister. I never did think I was going to make it to her burial and I didn't. The whole thing seemed redundant, but I continually asked her what she was going to say when she sees me the first time after that. I pretty much know. I can see her saying it now.

She says "I try very hard to leave it in God's hands."

A sense of justice gets me in trouble. Whose doctrine of fairness is fair?

"Love makes no record of wrongs," but justice does. Love is a pain we all bear, those who are lucky enough to get it.

The Handmade Silk Dress

She has a handmade silk dress that was in the attic wardrobe but has now been retrieved to the second story.

Frame it, I say.

No, she says, "I leave it in the closet, sometimes try it on."

That deepens my reverence.

Going to church is for her is like trying on this dress, a signature of the week, starts it off right.

On the downhill run different ministers have different goals. Faith leads to action which leads to attitude. But attitude gets bogged down.

"The religious are always behind the curve," she says, "can't realize that the past is the past. Call it what you will, everyone is so desperate to fit in, fit into the knowledge of the past, fit into the identity their schoolmates gave them, fit into the identity of their job, the host of other-centered conventions, conformity, the myth of their being."

McCommodate. McCommodate.

The flip side is that only when you fit in can you realize your destiny. Tradition is like trying on the handmade silk dress for her, becoming what you have become and finding it is like what your mother became. That brings back the past with a blast. But it saves from reductionism, from the lament of pathetic Robert Lowell, "stalled by the climacteric of his want." There is no stalling here, the car drives straight through into the after life without a hitch. She fulfills her destiny.

Anna Mack was cared for by daughter Anna Elizabeth in later years, but started insisting about 1965, "I'm not going to be a sweet old lady."

Now, forty years later the daughter chimes in. "He's a bore. His brother's a bore."
"I'm glad I'm named after you," I tell her.

But when the coals fly in my direction I keep a watchful distance.

She goes back and forth on being nice. When institutionalized she makes a steady credible effort to be nice to the help and to the visitor friends just because she doesn't feel so good. That's because it's easier to do the opposite of what you feel, at least it's more fun. She turns pain. The worse it is the more she doesn't show it. She has pain pills, a regimen, but because it's harder to be nice it appeals to her to do so. Also, it's a necessary survival technique, but she only takes aspirin. Living on Orange St. she could get real tired of being nice and would flay the edges with wit, because then, when there was no pain, that was harder, therefore more fun.

Yes the dress fits.

"I'm getting more like my mother every day."

Letting Go the House

She was still attached to that four story house she lived in for 60 years, whose sale the middle of March she survived by three weeks.

She wanted notes of appreciation from those who received her belongings and there were lots of questions. That house kept her busy.

"What happened to the tile tables, the silver? Where's the strawberry bowl? What happened to the *Thirty Thousand Immigrants* book I told you Jerry faxed John that he wanted. Well I guess I can't expect you to remember everything (anything!). Where's the genealogy?"

She made lists of questions on her bed at night and grilled me in the morning. I didn't tell her I wasn't going to the funeral, couldn't stand the thought of her rising up with more questions. John took the workbench. Joey got the kitchen table, the Sydenham chair. But half hadn't gotten anything yet. It sits in boxes on my porch awaiting the post. "Where's the china dog from the closet? Who has the crystal from the buffet, it's worth $150." Everything was up from being worth $100. The present age of everything became the 30's, but that too would change.

She was still attached to that body too. Hospice wanted to increase her pain meds, but the real pain was emotional and mental. Memory fading, old scores really needed feminine sympathy and care, pats on the hand and heart hugs when she lamented she had no daughter. She admitted when her niece Anne left she shed a tear, but said it was inside. By this time I was afraid to telephone her at all except I needed identities of some photos sent to her. I did call, three times, got a busy signal, a no answer, then an "I can't talk."

Attic and Basement

Her hard hat, hard edge perception and unsentimental eye beat Rimbaud in one thing, showed him how to sacrifice art for life, art for love and duty not for self
infatuation.

Her house has four levels. Each closet hides a world. The basement is galactic. The cleaned attic is the universe. But consciousness determines what we see and what we find, so likely there is more.

Search Ctrl plus F. The number four comes up twenty seven times as we inquire about four stories of her home. She lived mainly in the middle of those, but I was placed at the top in the attic in those childhood years. The analogy of the house to the four levels of interpretation, the attic mystical, bedrooms allegory, living room dining, kitchen morality and the basement literal is a discarded medieval order that offers itself as a sort of spaceship to take you away, even if Wittgenstein declares that the source of all thought and speech does not speak. You have to bunk where they put you. He will not say another word though and neither will Maimonides (*Guide of the Perplexed*) so we go to central theme of Marc-Alain Ouaknin (*The Burnt Book*) and Milton for the four Cherubic shapes" "flashing thick flames," a "wheel within wheel undrawn" and a multitude of eyes that run to and fro throughout, "rushing forth with 'whirlwind sound" to overwhelm the rebel angels in the culminating War in Heaven. That is maybe why the old men queue to go up above and below, but it won't surprise that she also has trapdoors built in the floor.

On wash days she would descend to the basement and go through boxes of her past on top of the dryer while waiting for the clothes. She wouldn't go to the attic. The steps were steeper and twice as many. Also there was no necessity. "It's dirty up there." In old age, the allegory reads, we can go down, but not up.

In the attic, where we came from in the allegory, repose the chests, old wardrobes, trunks, cookware from the woodstove, old German books, the show towels of ancestors inside trunks, bookcases stocked with poetry, pottery, blankets, files, her childhood rocker, the quilts, symbolic of pre-life and childhood experiences. Old men used to practically queue up just to spend an hour there, as if the smells, the dim light, the red wood, the open frame roof would cure them of age. With all the smugness of eternal delight I had them beat. The attic was where I used to sleep as a boy at age 5 under the red wood of the ceiling, the still life oils piled high on the tops of wardrobes out of reach.

The attic is up two flights, the basement is just one down. The old would settle for it, trading wood gables for stone and casement windows. The basement held the old wooden tools, the planes, levels, rasps, wooden screw clamps my oldest son brought away on many excursions, the wood aged with a dark patina. Here Marvin kept the luminous rocks he collected from all over SE Pennsylvania and the world, raw materials for his gates of the New Jerusalem: jasper, red and brown like the petrified woods of northern Arizona, amber, obsidian, garnets in quartzite, tan and white feldspar with quartz, green chrysogalla, milky quartz, fluorescent Deweylite, six sided tourmaline with mica, tan calcite with fluorescing pink franklinite crystals, white calcite with bornite and chalcopyrite, grey limestone with calcite, talc, speckled granite, shell fossils, jasper fossils, crustacean fossils, talc, lava, chalcopyrite with copper ore, i.e. Fool's gold, round balls of fiery garnets.

When I visited with my sons, 10 and 14, Marvin would disappear into the basement with them after dinner and go through the rocks for hours. He gave them stones for their gates. Then he gave about 40 boxes to the geological society. Years after his departure, there were still more rocks, plates of fern fossils stuck into padded mailing envelopes.

But there were bowls of buffalo nickels, jars of Indian head pennies under the old dining room table from Syndenham St. with the claw feet falling apart near the old wood stove from 1900, and the cabinet from antagonist grandfather, contrary Jake, who she said made it just to prove he could, and the chest Harvey Mack made for her when she lived in Ephrata in the 30's, with copious notes from all her trips abroad. More mundane things too, the storm doors and windows that I flew out to put up in the fall and then flew out again in the spring to take down. They were stuck up against the old coal bin, detailed images of the domestic Dutch, the old houses.

She had had a railing installed by a female carpenter down these basement steps because her feet were frail. In the years after the broken hip, the lost husband, the repaired cataract, the realist could have used the loaves and fishes, the water turned into wine. I longed to do this for her.

The best I ever did was when I sent my wife and son to visit and wrangled tickets to the old Barnes Museum, where she, the artist, had never been. Of course she told them she wouldn't go, but my wife rented a wheelchair and my son pushed her to the rented car, and up the Barnes elevator she went around the tiny rooms with their masterpieces as numerous as stars.

The English/German Cultural War

The Last Dutchman

The flowering heart is an image deep rooted in Pennsylvania German life. What it is, what it was in the history and biography of a culture, religion, family, and a person is the purpose here. The heart of these people gets ever more specific the closer we come to the person. Anna Elizabeth Reiff Young is the center of this effort. If we know a little of her from inferences gained in reading, being and seeing, we know the same of the greater family, her mother, her mother's people, their people, the Mennonites with the past and present of Pennsylvania German culture.

She was the last surviving Dutchman in a family of only Dutchmen for nine generations. Her idea of the rural, Dutch, peasant past conflicted strongly with the ideals she set for herself. She knew Latin, read literature, had an analytical mind and disdained parts of that culture as it deteriorated into the modern. She would sketch the past generations:

"My grandparents were farmers, but both my mother and my father had moved from Berks County to the city before they married in 1906. I was born in Philadelphia and attended Philadelphia schools, but I can claim all the virtues as well as the shortcomings of the Pennsylvania Dutch. One writer says 'they have their admirable features including frugality, tenacity and an extraordinary sense of community, but they can be irritating, petty and just plain thick headed as most of their neighbors will testify at length.'"

She, who was agonized by the stories of farm drudgery, poverty and cultural isolation, believed these things prevented her from being a physician. So conflicted by her perception of every positive and negative trait of her Pennsylvania Dutch identity she decided to be an artist.

To prove how Dutch a ninth generation last Dutchmen could be, she had given a talk on this heritage at a local high school years before. She wrote in a draft of this speech: "the human urge to create something beautiful has always given the world artists, composers, musicians, architects, furniture makers, dress designers and a long list of others who have spent their lives in the pursuit of beauty. Not the Pennsylvania Dutch! Their harsh existence kept them busy supplying the needs of family and community without much thought for beauty."

"In the pursuit of beauty… not the Pennsylvania Dutch," she was the artist, her grandfather and both his brothers musicians, her great uncle Andrew a cabinet maker, her mother a dress designer, her sister a scholar and author, her sister in law the daughter of an architect, a cousin by marriage a composer. Contradicted practically verbatim. The search for the beautiful and its conflict was a theme and counter theme to everything she did. Her artistic talent was noticed in 9th grade at Germantown High. She was one of two selected to attend the Philadelphia School of Industrial Art to do painting, clay modeling, carving, drawing, etc. She graduated high school at 15, entered the Moore Institute of Design for Women at 16.

"I was realistic enough to realize I wasn't a genius, only a medium talent. On the piano I could only play hymns for Sunday school. I'm very thankful to be realistic. I tell people I'm dying of cancer."

The presumed realism in "not the Pennsylvania Dutch" and "I wasn't a genius," is contradicted by fact. So is "I'm dying of cancer." The usual course of her malady was six weeks. It took her more than six months to die. After three months suspicious docs wanted more tests, but she would take no more tests. For pain killers she took aspirin.

There is an extraordinary musical aptitude in her background. Her grandfather, Henry Mack, was a "chorister and musical director in many [Mennonite] churches in this part of the state" (obituary). He and his brother Andrew Mack, the Mennonite bishop, had been choristers since 1860 (Wenger, 120). Likewise, their brother Peter was "an accomplished musician." Her brother, Howard, assistant VP of Bell, was a devoted lifelong chorister. Her cousin by marriage, Anthony J. Loudis, graduated Juilliard in 1928 in piano and composition, took advanced degrees at Columbia and was chairman of the University of Delaware music department. Another cousin, Noah K. Mack, M. B. E., physician graduate of Hahnemann Medical School in 1937, was a Mennonite medical missionary in Tanzania for 14 years, then the sole doc of Morgantown, Pa.

Her mother's family, the Macks had been teachers, pastors and musicians for generations, even-minded thoughtful men. Henry Mack had been a school teacher, as had his brother Peter Mack from 1860-1870. Peter and Andrew were both pastors as well, Lutheran and Mennonite respectively. All three brothers left their ideas in written form. Bishop Andrew Mack left 49 letters, 1870-1906, courtesy of the Jacob Mensch collection. Peter left a diary, 1870 until his premature death in 1878 (cited in *Souvenir History of Zion Lutheran Church*, 1753-1893). Henry kept detailed ledgers of his activities from the age of 21, 1875 until 1900. He also compiled the *Record of Tombstone Inscriptions / Old Mennonite Cemetery of the Hereford Congregation of Mennonites* (1934) an invaluable preservation of the identity of these early settlers.

Her sister was a groundbreaking author with a master's degree, chairman of home economics education of the Wilmington school district. Her great uncle Andrew Mack, the cabinet maker, was more importantly the most significant leader and diplomat for 19th century Mennonites. Her mother was a tailor and a woman of great independence and character, a Mennonite Mary Shelley instilling the rights of women in her daughters.

She was surrounded by excellence and thoughts of beauty.

The Cultural War

At the end of that talk she gave at Strathaven High School in 1991 she said, "as times have changed, we have stopped feeling inferior because of our peasant ancestry," meaning non-English. Her shame of peasantry, including folk art, stemmed from its indoctrination in her mind with farm ignorance and drudgery. But if she insisted that her people were peasants, they were not even pretend peasants.

To understand the complex psyche of Pennsylvania Dutch customs that poured out a decorated wave of chests, plates, linens and quilts, we have to understand how the shaming of English prejudice made them defensive and how this rejection of the body antagonized the artist's mind.

Much of this prejudice was not the native's own, it was fostered from the outside. The cultural cold war between the English and the German resembles that between the English and every other ethnic and racial group in America. In the case of the German the parody began in the dark faces, short thighs, and incomprehensible German tongues that antagonized Ben Franklin. The foreign had always antagonized the Puritans for whom the Indian was the first threat. The German was the second. An enlightened view of what lurked just beyond the fringe of consciousness of "decent" English civilization, just beyond the clearing's edge, considers that the Indians, wild men, and the dark unknown were really the personification of the Puritans' own sins, wolfishly portrayed. It was their own fear of themselves that they sought to keep from entering outposts and towns. This serious prejudice against themselves they transferred to the Indians and then to the Pennsylvania Dutch.

It's easy to be facetious about these attitudes. Her own defense against the oppression of peasant norms was caustic humor. This approach-avoidance to folk life was much the same as her ambivalence with the Mennonites. Calling herself "a mashed potato baby," she made it a negative myth of childhood that all her people were peasants with stubby fingers, thick thighs and heavy accents. This incremental rhetoric was still gaining momentum when she was in high school and she still felt vaguely suspect, implicated in the supposed German 5th column movements of W.W. I.

English loathing was translated in her saying, "mashed potatoes were a substitute for mother's milk for Pennsylvania Germans."

"They called me chubby baby."

"My legs were slightly uneven making me a little clumsy."

"I wasn't muscular."

"I was a mashed potato baby."

"I have peasant hands, short stubby fingers."

Neither Ben Franklin nor the puritan could appreciate that the Pennsylvania Dutch genius had domesticated nature, invited it indoors, befriended it on the hearth and loom and within human nature, and while they spoke little of it, they painted it and sculpted it, potted it and threw it on the forge. Thus domesticated, nature in

Pennsylvania didn't produce a *Scarlet* Letter or spooky stories, but decorated chests and barns. This erosion by the English of the way into the flowering heart was to produce an inferiority complex in these people whose pietistic ways were anyway hard to obtain, the silence of devotion, the acceptance of suffering, the union with God.

It wasn't even so much an inferiority complex as it was a shaming of the German to make them reject their identity. Such attempts have been made upon every ethnic and racial minority group in America. It may not be possible to name a native or immigrant group that the English have not so shamed. From the Welsh and Bengalis to the Irish, English prejudice has insinuated itself into places where English wasn't spoken.

She charges it against all of them. Even if the men of the Mack family were tall, slender and finely tuned, Grandfather Henry got it anyway.

"Henry had suits made to order. He was long from the waist to the knee, had heavy thighs."

But Henry was a lousy farmer.

"They weren't athletes."

She includes her other grandfather, defendant Jacob L. and his son, Howard, her father, storekeepers, "stocky, thick."

None of this is applied to the women much, except herself. "My family never had any growth spurts."

"It's an ethnic thing," she maintains. "I have a peasant body."

If you were a German peasant you were ridiculed as short, powerful and close to the ground. This was seriously engrained in her caricature so that she made sure to inform me that I was of peasant stock, that **I even looked like her father!** "Short legs and

powerful thighs are better for digging with shovels," not exactly what the boys crowed when I launched into the air with a terrible backhand poach into the deuce court. "The Great Wallenda!" they called, the German-American high wire founder of The Flying Wallendas who performed far above the ground. I was measured for vertical leap at a tennis match at age 60 at 26." Element of faculty vs. *Texas Monthly* softball game in Austin on Sunday where Ron Weddington and his law buddies also played called "Mr MoPac" where the MoPac freeway that bordered beyond the park where we played saw five home runs hit over the outfield's heads.

Ben Franklin was unable to fully retract his <u>letter to Peter Collison</u> of 1753 that - "in Europe, the Spaniards, Italians, French, Russians and Swedes, are generally of what we call a **swarthy** Complexion; as are the Germans also, the Saxons only excepted, who with the English, make the principal Body of White People on the Face of the Earth… the Number of purely white People in the World is proportionally very small" -where beside being tawney, "Those who come hither are generally of the most ignorant **Stupid**

Sort of their own Nation, and as Ignorance is often attended with Credulity when Knavery would mislead it, and with Suspicion when Honesty would set it right; and as few of the English understand the German Language, and so cannot address them either from the Press or Pulpit, 'tis almost impossible to remove any prejudices they once entertain." Franklin was offended by the immigrants who arrived in the 1750s, for by then Franklin, down from New England, had naturalized in Philadelphia from that purer society and had been profusely printing some of the most provocative thought of the colonies of Conrad Beissel, *Ninety Nine Mystical Sentences* (1730) and Michael Wohlfahrt (1737) and multiple editions of hymns until he was supplanted by the German printer Christoph Saur. Of course Franklin, grand master of Pennsylvania Masons, lived in London thereafter, from 1757-75, on Craven St, where, refurbishing his residence for a museum 15 bodies including six children were found buried from that time in a secret, windowless room beneath the garden, oh foolish Galatians. To speed these retractions therefore before worse appears, when the weightlifters of San Jose I visited in the company of Ricardo Foulkes, the concert pianist of Costa Rica, kept asking in admiration where did I get my legs, I said, "at birth."

The Pennsylvania German mind, all along the target of the English cultural war, degraded by association made short thighs equal the short mind, not supplied with cardinal virtue, but with retrograde stubbornness, pride and separateness, "irritating, petty and just plain thick headed," symbolized in the house frau, *die Mem*, the rough skinned farmer's wife.

Apple in the Attic

This brutishness occurs in a book from Libby's library, *Apple in the Attic: A Pennsylvania Legend* (1942), whose heroine Emma doesn't know she is pregnant. All the stereotypes of brutish husbands and calloused hands fail in the language and customs of the English/German cultural war. *Apple* replayed in homes across Pennsylvania from the doll Flora wanted (165) to the Mother who wants even more to give it to her, to the hands, "tools of a farmer's wife…not a woman's hands, for they were too gross to be gentle" (144), gave the message flee the farm. Anna Mack got out as soon as possible. She later produced dolls galore for her daughter, who of course cared little for them, being a realist by age 10.

Elizabeth and Anna were together in the front ranks of the rights and equality of women, but Emma's child Flora was the very person she abhorred, "brought up on pap as a baby, soon graduated to sauerkraut and pretzels" (134). So while the novel panders to stereotypes and Emma in her attic of seclusion in (real time, 1942) finds justification for the stereotypes in her own experience it had absolutely nothing to do with Anna Elizabeth.

That would-be physician never spoke a word in dialect, nor did her mother or grandfather, but there was one exception, the stepmother, *die mem.* Henry Mack had remarried after losing Elisabeth Longacre Bechtel. His second wife was everything a stepmother is feared to be. Anna, the only daughter of that family and the oldest, bore *die mem's* government. In Emma's words, "stop your vashing to change again zem didies" (122), takes the part for the whole, but Anna was imbued with her Mack forebearers, gracious musicians and teachers. *Die mem* had two sons with Grandfather Henry after Elisabeth Bechtel died, but if they achieved the thick and stout, had to be forgiven because they were very smart and principled men, Philip Mack the millionaire, Harvey Mack, celebrated for fulfilling his Mennonite vocation as an ambulance driver in WWI and afterward as a carpenter in the reconstruction of France.

It is to mock prejudice that higher intelligence jokes upon people who boast they are peasants born of peasants as far back as

Charlemagne. They are teasing you, looking down their nose to see if you are gullible enough to believe it. Aping the naïf has been good business since the Impressionists. It pleases artists to go native for its own sake who even in poverty have no doubt they are the true aristocrats who hear and see that every bird that cuts the airy way is an immense world of delight compassed by your senses five (Blake). The claim of aristocrats of mind and sense to peasant hood is always a put on. Sure, her grandfather, Henry Mack, did a tour on the farm. But her mother, Anna, escaped and this daughter never milked a cow.

Reconcile the Paradox

Reconcile these paradoxes and you have case in point, a last Dutchman with nine generations of vested folk identity and an artist, trained and meticulous, who negates both. Doesn't that make her more interesting than if had she affirmed both? You can see the conflict circling around. Of course she denies both in interesting ways because neither folk nature nor the credentials of artistic eye and mind ever go away. Shame and prejudice is directed against all living contradictions of ourselves, our families and our physical and mental beings. To excavate the real folk beneath we cannot entirely believe the reports given us. The details themselves, in context, give us a shot at reconstructing the life that was, and better able to solve the life that is.

Like a parable in a Henry James story, a mystery even if we explain it away, or the supposed Shakespearean authorship of Psalm 46 translated in the King James Version, there are parallels in the Sonnets and the Plays that support the idea of his translation of this psalm, leaving his signature if you count 46 words from beginning and end, but the supposed facts belie the most obvious, that in the English translations before 1611 that King James "code" was just a word or two from being sprung. So if it isn't a mystery it's an even greater literary accident. So basements and attics of the house metaphor and the self are filled with facts that must be extracted as inferences on the floors between. Were it not for research and memory we know only the unconnected.

The Mind of Domestic Particulars: Redeeming Nature in Folk Art

The attempt to denature folk of their ethnicities faced a counter offensive that celebrated the folk as they truly exist. So the extraordinary celebration of the good in the natural of the Dutch and their domestication of nature in the images and creations of folk life that the English feared.

The history of the middle class imitating their upper class betters is much to the point of a desire for the beautiful among these people of whom it is said that, "peasants, burghers and common men move toward nobility by adopting in their own way, the sumptuousness of the upper classes. Their copies of upper-class wares, from furnishings to portraits to attire, are frequently grouped together under the name of folk art…for the first time objects inscribed with their owners' names" (Weiser, *The Decorated Pennsylvania Chest*, 13). But more important even than folk art imitating nobility, art must imitate life, which folk art did without pretense.

Anna Mack had conflict with plain style over the proper nature of dress. She fled the Dutch accents and the thought that education was worldly, a kind of heroine of peasantry. In the city she became a tailor, made the high boned collar, the leg mutton sleeve, the tiny waist, the wide lined skirt. Anna's brother, Jesse Mack, a six foot redhead, singer and artist also sought escape, but he died tragically at 26. One impasto watercolor of his remained, labeled "valuable" in a folder in her desk, but just as the roosters and weathervanes were coming apart, in the settling of her estate it was lost.

When writers refer to the bygone 18th century Pennsylvania German imagination as a retrospective for the "lily age," they mean that the symbolic images of the hymns, gardens, artifacts and décor mutually exposit an internal state of mind not talked about and for that reason all the more real. Christ is the lily, his human nature the rose (101), but the lily is also the believer in a compounding paradise, "uncontaminated good with natural reality." (Stoudt, 101). These generations, as Mennonites were prone, said little about their faith, thinking such celebration worldly, of the ego, but they went about day to day contemplating the eternal in temporal and often floral images. Out of this Stroudt claims for the Pennsylvania Dutch "the first indigenous folk art in America" (xviii).

Where did she get her mind? Visited in her sanctuary of last retreat in Life Care and apprehended in reading the biblical text, one did not ask what she read. Speech about the holy was imperiled, but the least insight demonstrates that her identity was so based. Where did she get her mind? From the inescapable lily, in other words, the universal Pennsylvania Dutch "tulip," which is really a lily in the iconography of PA German folk art. Though it looks like a tulip, indeed, we would say that it is a tulip, that is not what the artists themselves say of it. (Stoudt, 106). They say it is Christ.

Good In the Natural

Good in the natural hugely impacts the conflict of body and soul in the Pennsylvania Dutch. To say there is an uncontaminated good in the natural completely contradicts essential Calvinism and Puritan thought. But the good within the natural and natural events is a dominant theme in the Pennsylvania Dutch decoration of household objects and in their Pietistic thought. So while they are a plain people on the outside in terms of their dress, their inner lives, imaginations, are ornate.

Direct access to this occurs especially in folk art. Such things were not going to be spoken of even if they were sung. There is not going to be much conversation about the Lily who is praised in song and art. That the Pennsylvania German is so heavily medieval in praise of Christ also explains the continuing diffidence of modern scholarship, which like the "inarticulate belief in the artist's heart" (Stoudt, 15) has remained pretty quiet about examining this artistic, devotional, religious iconography.

As far as it goes the boast made by Stroud still holds good. The Pennsylvania Dutch "produced an American decorative art which, with few minor exceptions, is the only indigenous art of its kind in our land" (3). The lily "dominates the poetry and the literature; tulips appear rarely in verbal form."

She got the garden and home of her mind from this milieu, but the prejudice against the body from biographical and fictional sources like *die mem* and *Apple in the Attic*. Body and mind were in mortal conflict all her life and always with the proviso that one should not reveal the inner life. That would be pride. One must disdain the flesh. "There was no "self-expression" in the religious folk art of Eastern Pennsylvania for one who insists upon having their own way, either in art or in life, is an egotist" (Stoudt, 9-10). This is fundamental Mennonite theology as well, so if there is a refrain in her life, especially whenever she doubted or was suspicious of the motives of another or herself, it was against egoism. Of course the whole issue of the self submerged in tradition and thus masked is endemic to art. The greatest freedom is freedom from oneself.

We must recognize that these collective biblical images underlay her mind with health, courage and faith. But the mind is not separate from the body or from the emotions. We may say that the mind is to its surroundings and upbringing as folk art is to its tradition. So if Pennsylvania German folk art receives its meaning from the literary tradition which accompanies it, her mind received meaning from the surrounding culture portrayed not only in the artifacts, but also in the family tradition that is the literary Pennsylvania German, the Bible, German medieval and Pietistic hymnody and Pennsylvania German hymnals. They say art was not favored in Mennonite families. But that is disproved by the "tulips" embroidered in the celebration of the Pennsylvania Dutch soul.

Works Cited

Mildred Jordan. *Apple in the Attic.* A Pennsylvania Legend. NY: Knopf, 1942.

John Joseph Stoudt. *Pennsylvania German Folk Art.* Allentown, PA: Schlechter's, 1966.

Frederick S. Weiser in *The Pennsylvania-German Decorated Chest* by Monroe H. Fabian. Atglen, PA: Schiffer Publishing Ltd..

J. C. Wenger. *History of the Mennonites of the Franconia Conference.* Telford, PA: Franconia Mennonite Historical Society, 1937. Republished by Mennonite Publishing House. Scottdale, PA, 1985.

The first Century of German Language Printing in the United States of America. Volume 1 (1728-1807).

Poems on Cans

I get hold of her by phone right before the cleaner is to come, expect a slam- down, but the cleaner doesn't show so we rationalize why the neighbor's Pekinese when sheared won't come out on the porch, but our black chow shivers in the Phoenix heat.

Of course, I argue, dogs, at least our dog, eats better than most people.
"People food is better, but you have to read the label."
"Read the label! What's on them, poems?"

I suspect Mennonite millennial billboards to read "Just say no to Pride." The clothing labels, cereal boxes will have a message. She's been reading labels ever since the beginning because they didn't have enough books. She read the shredded wheat box, volume after volume. It had pretty pictures, strawberries, Niagara Falls.

"It's too bad you didn't keep those boxes, they'd be worth hundreds on the Internet."
"I don't save for worth, only for sentiment and use. The wrapper she gave me Henry Mack's journal in, an early and rare example of the plastic bag, has a large red scoop on its cover against a checkered yellow background. It reads, above and below,

BULK FOODS
SCOOP UP THE SAVINGS

Who would know better about the labels, she's a retailer.
My favorite poem label told to my mother-in-law made her break down laughing. You have to say it right, drawing out the syllables of the first word:
"L E A V E S.
Adam had'em."

It had snowed 3 inches in 3 hours. We revisit aphorisms and facts by phone: Howard II, grey eyes, ruddy complexion, Anna dark brown eyes, Flo, black hair and very fair skin. Father Howard on bill paying: "don't spend more than you have."

She's got a yen for fried potatoes, peeled, cut thin, cooked crunch brown and chewed with salt and pepper, still has a tendency to over-buy, then has to throw things out. Her plan for recycling is, "throw it out when the green things get brown and the brown gets green."

She doesn't remember the boned chicken her mother served at Sunday dinners, "that's because I got the bones." But Anna deboned all the chicken by hand, made her coffee very strong by measuring the water and boiling it, adding a measured amount of coffee till it boiled up with an egg in the bottom, then turned off the heat and put on a lid.

Where does measuring come in? The cherry pies were made with very red fresh sour pie cherries and had much sugar added. Anna had to pick the cherries from a tall ladder because she was light and strong on Henry's farm in Clayton. Small farm means just that, no acreage is assigned. Then she admits she can't eat cinnamon buns with a clear conscience.

Banquet

People worry about old ladies in snow storms and their pantries since there has been no shopping for ten days. She says that she can "make the dish," a coinage from the 30's when she traveled and took a room with the rudiments. Into the one allowed pan went tomatoes, ground beef and rice with seasoning. She had the dish last week. There is also tuna fish, spaghetti. My Welsh-speaking wife overnights gourmet crackers two kinds of cheese, a large bar of chocolate. Oranges and grapefruit, a bi-monthly event, are already ordered. The Dutch like to eat. In Phoenix, debating Christmas dinner, whether salmon, roast or Mexican, she volunteers, salmon on Christmas Eve for the Italian, roast on Christmas day for the English and Mexican the day after.

Spend many isolated but important moments in a life but combine them into one day and the 30 seconds or five minutes of consciousness ignited in that day equals the mortal span. The rest of the time, the theory goes, we are going round the grill looking at shadows that these images cause on the wall, lost in the particular. What is there to think about anyway, memories, the dolls we had to play with, meals and the recipes?

Shoofly

Shoofly is heavy in molasses. Molasses and syrup were put onto paper rolls on strips that hung above the tables with the pies to catch the flies. Hence shoo, fly.

My Wittgenstein, it is worth something to stay alive, an end in itself. She's living well, for breakfast had half a grapefruit, a dish of shredded wheat, bananas and strawberries (from Florida), coffee and toast! Has gained three pounds with all the lack of action from the weather.

I respond I like half an onion charred in olive oil with a small piece of deer sausage and brown rice, cayenne pepper on top. She says cayenne wouldn't agree with her belly, sweet in the belly if hot in the mouth.

Free at last from the low sodium, low fat foods she gave Marvin, she lives on carbs, has helped Alan Alda, who took a 3

month fat trial on TV, video his belly, then show a fat operation
where they cut the stomach and the fat. Lovely thing. *Throw down
your mattock and dance while you can.*

Video inside the belly and what will you see? You really just
need a goal. And a camera.

Of the varieties of cookie and fruit tart by mail she says she
was not aware they were outsourcing the raspberry to Indonesia.
Then there were the Dare Cookies, a new cookie distributed by
Global Cookies made in Canada.

As a chaser to all your tales take fruit juice on your cereal,
cranberry on shredded wheat.

Robert, Cynthia, Laura visit. It provokes a mutual interest in old
things. No pun, but it doesn't matter whether you go to attic or
basement or anywhere in-between it's all old, a legitimately antique
life to boot. Laura is interested in gardening and canning, a pint of
apple butter "made the old way over a copper kettle and stirred all
night."

"I'm not devoted to apple butter."

But Laura's friend had apples, so turned loose in the basement,
she wanted the canning jars, the old-fashioned tinted ones that
Grandma used that had been boxed up, the ones with the zinc tops.
This was on Saturday. On Sunday when they came Laura made them
into 2 boxes and flew them away. Last night she called New Orleans
to see if the jars had passed safely into their new life. Does anybody
get this wry stuff?

Pork and Sauerkraut

This leads to a consideration of pork and sauerkraut, that
Pennsylvania German mainstay:

Marvin: cook in a pot on top of the stove.

Bea: in oven large baking dish, put meat in center. Center up
pork chops not cut apart in oven, 2 ½ to 3 hours with mashed
potatoes. Piece of "country ribs" and can of sauerkraut.

Marge has some apples in it and seasoning.

"But the way we, Grandma did it, didn't need a recipe."

Weaknesses yet to be purged to reach the next level of austerity
include milk in jasmine tea, "...not sweet things, no milk, no sugar, a
little lemon juice occasionally."

Marvin liked red tea and mint.

Her father had a sweet tooth for the caramelized halves of
grapefruit and orange; he'd cut them the night before and put an
eighth inch of sugar on each half, by morning they were ready.

She puts seedless grapes on her cereal. This justifies the
menu police. Acme has white, red and black (from Chile) grapes. No
doubt they have their eye on her at Acme after the grape juice
situation. She cuts these grapes in half and puts 2 or 3 on her cereal.
She likes the surprise when you open the refrigerator: "they are
almost as big as a small date, like the huge bunch of grapes the spies
in Canaan found."

This leads to a parable:
> Once a cloned giant who lived in a grape,
> was dry and turned into an ape.

Church dinner, ½ in a cake. Raisins and olives. Strawberries.

Bruce is being given steroids, had his first radiation today which is to run 5 days a week for 4 weeks. He wears a knit cap to protect the incision which goes over the left eye into the hairline.

"One rose is enough" she says.
> She got the citrus we sent on Sat.
> Bruce can't eat citrus.
> She can't peel the orange skin, it's too thick.

Now you know what real problems are. Tying shoes, putting on socks, peeling citrus. But no nuts for the last 25 or 30 years because she gets diverticulitis. "I love nuts" she says, pecans and walnuts, curved nuts, cashews.

Anna made salted almonds, a rite because you had to shell them. With the dark skin of the nut removed you would boil them and pop them from the skin, dry, and put in a flat pan with butter and salt. Bake a short time.

Celery is bad for her too, along with almonds. The cure was to stop everything for a week. Everybody though has these problems with Brussel sprouts, rhubarb.

After Christmas

She allows driving in the daylight, doesn't like living alone, cooks three nights a week. On the list of infirmities she is a little hard of hearing. I suggest that she get a voice projector as a sideline. Coffee in the morning.

Bessie Collins in S.F. drank tea. The counter man was disgusted when she said, "I take tea." For Lib it's orange green tea, but make it weak. Why not, I suggest, a blend of black and green tea.
Has she heard of the new long liver's tea made of apricot pits?

No.
They used to call these kinds of things monologues.
"You've got three months to rationalize '03."

Her answer is *toot suite*. She says she has a Christmas tree this year. It is 3 in. tall with burlap at the base covered with little lights.

She has boiled it down, remains sappy in life, more vibrant than she could wish, surrounded by gargantuan packages of crackers and a dozen kinds of tea with her own handmade mug. When she was a girl they got just an orange some years, but now the oranges and grapefruits are bigger. So is she in spirit. One other present, another expensive floral arrangement from Bruce.

We range back and forth among the nieces and nephews. When I tell her we are considering sending our 8th grader to college she says, "they need time to mature," as if we're in the produce department. Probably the best reason to do this is so he can get enough sleep. High school is such a waste of time.

It is 26 degrees.

She says she "could hardly bear to open" the packages of crackers and tea, wrapped individually with the Japanese tea cup with the mid-red splotch of Indian color from the southwest, thrown by Eden. She is impressed with Aeyrie's pen and ink of hills and landscape, very b & w, "simple" she says, "with great feeling, it's amazing. It gives a feeling of space, that's rare."

New Year's Resolution: "Be thankful is my resolution," she says, "for what I've got and not complain about what I've not."
I don't burden her with my poem "By the tankful."

She's got Aeyrie's art and Andrew's thank you note all brilliant in pastels to keep her company. But she's got more arthritis in the right hand so her own thank you notes are unwritten. Her Hindu doctor has the Hippocratic notion of don't do damage so she's sticking with the aspirin and Advil of the stone age.

Winter

"How are you?"

"Medium."

"How do you like your meat?"

"I don't eat meat much anymore".

"How about prime rib?"

(Chuckles) "Medium rare. I like it but it tastes bad later in my teeth and belly."

"How old do you think I am anyway?"

"62."

"Not chronologically, really."

"Don't make me think."

The weather is snow, she can't go out, gets "stir crazy and nervous." I tell her I hate January. It's cold, dark, no sun and all you can do is lay on the couch and read the *Nibelungenlied*. February's just as bad and March! (except in AZ)

She's answered letters from two people, a little late, a year or two behind. The woman who took care of Marvin's sister and her estate, very competent and friendly. She got a letter from grand niece Elizabeth, a thank you note, where E. says she is saving her money to go to Scotland in March. The temperature's going up, the ice melted, then refroze last night.

Notes and lists are put in their place.

On her brother visiting old people all the time, which both she and he did, it is not a ministry. "I didn't have a nursing home ministry, (at least not regularly)." She would read publicly one or two times a month at specified times, on a schedule. She doesn't say, but I know from priors, that she rehearsed these meticulously.

In Media they're putting in winter pansies. Bruce sent her a floral arrangement for Christmas which she hates, it contradicts the surrogate nature of her anti-gardening because you have to water it every day. Also there's a problem in how to get rid of them.

Down to the bone.

Function/Form

Cramming for March exams doesn't always help, she says, so maybe the fact that youngest son Andrew has been sick for several days and in bed doesn't mean he's not prepared for the tournament in El Paso tomorrow. He stays sick, loses one match. In the final of the back draw he has lost the first set, is down 5-2 in the second, but wins it against an arch rival who has had him on the ropes before but never won. He finishes the third at 7-5.

I ask him at the break between the second and third, why are you keeping me here?

Aeyrie brought home a ceramic rattle he made, functionless I say, but that's art.

She used to go on her buying trips to NY alone by choice. One time, in the depression era, when metal was scarce and much experiment was being done in glass (Blanco) and ceramics she entered a store when another buyer entered simultaneously, but with a clipboard and two assistants to look at one piece. "It has no function" he said, and stomped out.

They used to sell lots of ashtrays, one for every room of the house at least and several for the living room. These and flower containers were plentiful so she told her girls that if a customer asks you about something and you don't know what it is tell them it's an ashtray or a vase.

But everybody knows that art is for art's sake, "otherwise why would they have little children dress up as ants in their church musical and hop around the building."

"Go to the ant." I don't say, "go to Aunt," for she is receiving continuing attentions from her now almost 97 year old "boyfriend." I guess that's pretty common nowadays, liking older men.

She says one more time that she's going to send the Henry Mack bio back with notes. One paragraph, needs to be omitted. Focus is everything. Granite doesn't lie. The accolade hurts, "I like it very much."

Staying up late today, being serially snowed in, for the Philadelphians of February '03 the good news is that your feet, which like to be cold, are cold, but this prevents the wash and the shopping. Julia, the latest driver, calls for the Tuesday shop, but 16 inches are on the ground. She says her car is poorly and the snow is deep.

Mennonites are as used to snow as they are to plain dressers, though most of those are gone now, replaced by couples rubbing one each other's necks in church. These rubbers are also become plain speakers.

To Julia:
"I can't tell you what to do with your car and I can't tell you what to do with the snow, but I can tell you what to do with yourself, go in and stay in and keep warm!"

Folk

The daylilies are blooming. She asks, "are there any doubles," that is 12 petals instead of 6? Yes. The double daylilies came from Uncle George's (1846-1932) place." The daylilies reach back further than the letters and are as soon gone, except that, paradoxically, there are both doubles and singles.

Folk Lilies

Some time ago she expunged her garden, dug the daylilies, stepped down the peppermint. African violets are still offending on the sill, and oh how the perennial body remains in bloom though it's more trouble not to look 100 where you're 94. This is a number to the onlooker, but to the subject gone without a perm in 6 months, instead of 4, it's ordeal. To the comment that none of the sports gurus have said boys should not compete during or immediately after growth spurts, she categorically asserts that there were "no growth spurts in my family." Eat a lot, sleep a lot, that's a growth spurt. She does them both.

Elk Sing

These are the questions of this November day, 2003, rising like Bambi from a forest fire. I ask, thinking it's a *non sequitur*, why would the Mennonite hunt elk?

"Well they hunted animals in the wood." The owl, twit twoo-woo. Woodpeckers. Yoga. I only transcribe what is written.

How to make trouble for yourself....

If in any way I am, is it because of me or because of it?

What is the inner self speaking out loud? Let everything that has breath praise Him.

And green tea, what does it do for you?

Milk in tea not sweeteners. She drinks ordinary tea and peppermint. Green tea with orange pekoe.

Do you want a little more spice in your life?

She is depressed. Albert, her first boyfriend, was going to teach her chess.

I had wanted to fire her up with the current Prayer of Confession of the Reformed. a twofer for sins but without the part in brackets:

"for the moodiness and irritability that makes us difficult to live with,"

[Lord have mercy on us]

"for the insensitivity that makes us careless of the feelings of others,"

[Lord have mercy on us]

"for the selfishness that makes life harder for others,"

[Lord have mercy on us]

"when we think of ourselves and of the meanness and ugliness and weakness of our lives…

[Lord shut us up.]

It's like a modern translation of *I Corinthians* in reverse where depression takes the place of immorality. Confess sins and rerepent every laborious week in the bulletin, cornerstone of depression. Where is desperation that leads to rescue? They foreshadow the demographic. There are soon to be large numbers of aging and dying people. The most greatest danger is to be between them and their sorrows.

A couple weeks before this they had a mission Sunday:

"Take a few moments to think of areas where you are involved or would like to be involved. Write down those commitments below and either place them in the offering plate…or take it home as a reminder."

I wrote one down but took it to the church coffee hour and confessed to the people, "I am committed to seeing and immersing all human agencies into the divine." I told Doug that I'd go to the state fair but there's too many people. He says, I like the people. Me, since I'm also transcribing letters of the past century, "the dead people are all around me." Maybe that didn't come out right. Age spends more time with the dead just below the surface of the minds. I'm going to call them the eternal.

I sent her one part of a five part poem, a sing between coyote and elk, Elk and Aspen, (*Frigg*, Spring / Summer 2022) written from trips to the White Mountains from 1986 until finished. She responds, "on the first reading I like this. It's not the sort of thing...it's poetry, not doggerel." She read it twice and it held its own. That's what the editors who published it said, "This work is incredible, but I wasn't quite sure what to make of it ... mostly because I feel like I'm going through a time when my attention span is short. I asked Dennis Mahagin, Frigg's poetry editor, to read it and let me know what he thought, and he said he LOVED it. He said, "In a hunter's milieu, a man hacks at some trees with language a sanctuary against death. The poem had rewards in store for a diligent reader. Those last five lines kill it." (He means "kill it" in a good way.) All I can say, I guess, is that the poem is beautiful, which is enough ... more than enough."

The final test, read aloud, will occur with the proviso that there are no coyotes in Media. She said she couldn't read the second part aloud because it needed a male voice. My male voice has gotten me in trouble in a radio. At the rehearsal for the Cutting Edge, Marty, my associate and his wife Mary, freaked. I use a voice similar to Goliath's for Archy, the Database Angel (Soundcloud). Andrew and Aeyrie are afraid of it.

Don't send any more, she said. It was coming onto Christmas and she had taxes to get ready for and thank you notes. The 94 years ruminate that she used to live in a women's world, she now lives in a man's. Dave Jeffers, one of her ex-drivers, who took care of his mother at the end of her life at 95, calls her as often. Then there's Jim, her newest and excellent driver, manly, full of wit and help. Bruce, Marvin's son, visits Saturdays. Ed does the grass. Charlie, the bus driver and transportation deacon with the senior construction committee from church does repairs etc., and her lawyer, tax man and sycophant, John, who will graduate to almighty confidant in the last days.

You'd think somebody who can be as abrupt with her nephew could carry it over to her great nephew Aeyrie, "content to fit in the background," she says she insists he should be a doctor, but won't tell him.

"You weren't so inhibited when you told me all the time as a boy that I had surgeon's fingers!
You weren't inhibited when you taught me how to wiggle my ears!"

Her reply, "I can't touch the tip of my nose with my tongue anymore."

So much for Mother's Day. In the old days when she was in the "second Christmas" greeting card business day, For Mom, I used to mock her that is, retailing.

Women and Mother's Day

I've just come from Mother's Day with the Conservative Mennonites. The men are going to cook for the women this evening, but the morning sermon is heavy with allusion that wives should be submissive, beauty not being outward. Invoking male leadership on Mother's Day can't be celebratory for a mother who married with one thing in her mind, hopes for the realization of her dreams. Thirty years later it comes down to petty fiefdom? What about the thing that got them there, even if you have outlived your youth, do you remember what started the ball? Well it was love! You've got to love that 50 year old woman like you did and more.

Contradictions. The mothers are important because they beget the sons who become the fathers. Her father Howard R. was an only child, a heavy burden, but his mother died. So which is worse, the mother that says she treated the only child like a child because he acted like child, or the son who says he acts like a child because she treated him like a child?

More children is the cure. But Howard's mother was deceased and he was the continuing only child because all the others died. Everybody liked him. Minnie, his second stepmother, said with tears at Howard's death, "why couldn't the Lord have taken me instead of Howard?" Jake had bought a car but didn't drive. Howard was his chauffeur, Sundays and otherwise, but Howard truly enjoyed the car in itself, refers to it in letters often enough. He also used it for good works in picking up people for church, driving Lib and JH to their various occasions. But all they can say of Jake is that he was hard on his wives.

Jake's sisters worried about him, especially at the end, called Libby to stop by on Saturday, but he died Friday night. Aunt Sue was already there, putting in his teeth, woman's work, caring for the living and the dead. Aunt Sue got to 96.

Senior Class

Sometimes, in jest, she said she wanted to be a professor.
"What kind, art?"
No answer.
Teasing, "home ec.?"
Snort.
"History?"
Now mocking.
 "No, English!"

"My friends went to Normal School to be teachers. I knew I wouldn't be patient with the slow."

The flow of information is sometimes complicated by illness, old age and confidence levels. Feeling strong one day, isolated from problems past and present, she says that everything in the house is in order. Confronted later by a disaffected claimant she has doubts, recriminations, fears, tensions hard to bear at any time, but when you're in the process of dying, harder. She will fire darts then at a near safe target, someone she believes could never injure her. Love hopes all things, endures all things, a hard message to recriminate.

Holy Feet

Our youngest son has slender feet: "all my family had slender feet, I was AAA. Your father had long slender fingers, I have plumpish ones (a Dutch dumpling!). He had braces too."

She mentions arthritis. I say again, I don't believe in it.
"You mean it was created by the medical profession?"
 "Or the drug industry"
"What about the rheumatism old people used to get."

"Old people get stiff but it can be treated. I'd massage and anoint them with lavender, pray for them while I was doing it. Heat packs. Ice packs. Stretch. Because I believe they'd get better they would. I am a placebo. I guess you think that borders on the holistic."

"I think you've gone the whole way over."

I tell her the belief that the thing is so, is so. I can quote Blake. Shall I? She says she doesn't believe in miracles. I call miracles subcutaneous, that dreaded word among females. Does the firm persuasion of a thing make it so, make it so?

You believe in healing? "Yes and no."

Earlier she had said she has prayed for me. I tell her I prayed for her too, that she would be "green and supple in old age" after the Psalm, notwithstanding Abraham's and Hannah's fertility, say "I'm just after the general health benefits for you."

"Thank you."

The bad weather came out of Grandma's knee and feet.

"I love you dear."

I love you too.

Senior Class

Know this about the Senior class, when it sounds just like they are about to graduate if they say they don't want to they won't. She won't remember today what "Media" means, even though the sign is just across the street. Some place in Egypt.

Reconstructing from notes, Bruce has been diagnosed with a brain tumor, is undergoing further treatment to dissolve it. He is not in as good spirits about it. She worries when he vacillates between being an old man or not by his gait. The hoodlums at the corner say don't hunch, lengthen your stride, walk from the hips or we will take you for a ride. Always pretend you're an athlete.

She's feeling nice, meaning in danger and in the mood to please, but never liked the rich.

"Why, don't they recognize royalty?"

This day of Abraham is either a decade or lasts a thousand years. She's an early bloomer blooming late, went to art school at 16, married at 72; at 92 with a new lens surgically implanted she could see color again in the tile floor.

In Upper Providence Township you need a certificate of occupancy and a rewiring certificate to sell, but even if you sold where would you go, she muses, to assisted or to independent living? Her area has the highest percentage of old folks outside of Texas. She's too old for assisted living, or too young. There are drawbacks to assistance. You have to line up to get medication in the health center and you can sit anywhere in the dining room unless the independents have reserved it, then you have to sit with the invalids. It's like high school.

She knew Andrew Mack and Aunt Lizzie when she was 8 or 9, remembers them when they were old, especially Aunt Lizzie confined to her room then, but with a covered glass dish with wintergreen pink candies to offer to children. She could make small talk to the children in English.

She's like her father, didn't want to be any trouble to anybody. Aunt Sue was 96, Aunt Mary 95.

"I want to outlive you."

"I'm more afraid of lasting too long than not.

"I'm willing to come out there and run your life!"

"I don't want anybody to run my life."

It's primary election day. She is waiting on the porch for a ride to the polls, says, "we talked about age, never about sex."

I ask, "what did they say?" "I don't want to talk about it."

So the timeline of inquiry is investigative, a universal present more than a chronology for this clandestine soul confined when all her life she was free.

Happy Hour

She was no flapper, but defends wine for a day. Marvin made it in the basement, but didn't think it should be taken before dinner. These are the things that matter. Larry and Bea had wine before dinner, before and after marriage, happy hour extended courtesy of Fitzgerald. But she has been "brainwashed." Oh we can talk about brainwashing. Get the brain washed and the body dry cleaned.

Her brother got married the year prohibition ended, 1934. Before that he lived at home, mortified at coming home drunk in front of his mother, but "never enough to change his behavior." Rudy, his buddy, older than he, and Choir Director John Wyand, were instrumental at First Mennonite in leading lapses into the bottle. After leaving the terrestrial, Bea's greatest fun was to have eight or nine "girls" over to her room on Wednesdays for glasses of wine and giggling.

Never a drinker, now fast a teetotaler, in the hospital with a broken hip, her suite mate had a psychiatrist analyze the suite mate at the behest of a boyfriend. She admitted she had been drinking and fallen even before this time. Since breaking her own hip this one won't even think drink. Thinking drinking, aiding and abetting, I say, "poison." At Chancellor Park, her hip rehab gig, they had happy hour, 4 to 5 every day, an open bar. She always meant to go, but somehow never made it., but she did the watercolor hour, never mentioning any priors. They hung one of these in the hallway.

Sorting Out The Past

Labor Day again, she is sorting out the basement on top of the dryer. It sounds like a line from a poem. She says all your life you accumulate decades of things so that in your old age you can go through them and throw them away.

No part of her day would be complete without a good read, no matter whether with magnifying glasses or the other kind. She reads collections of realism, Lewis Thomas' interpretation of physical things in a literary sense. A good realist subscribes to the *Smithsonian.*

She lives alone and doesn't get much chat, not like in the institution where carolers are ten deep and the phone rings. It is possible to talk too much to some people. Knowing who is the trick, get skilled at being nice, avoid the boring, scary loons and find the witty forgiving, no gossips.

Anybody can visit old ladies.

She watches Antiques Road Show. Her plastic bags are rare. She should frame all the lovely things she has. I saw one: BULK FOODS, with a grid and a scoop and the logo "SCOOP UP THE SAVINGS." The date on this bag was 1811! The dust in her attic is serious enough, the crumbling masonry. One day when plywood is rare I will cash in the many sheets on my porch.

The dutiful daughter loathes characterization, but is fed up with her third West African driver in as many months, says that maybe she's not a fighter per se. It's better to agree, then over-agree.

"You're right. How about we call you 'a stickler,' a 'feisty stickler'? You could get it made into a bumper sticker." "I'd have to wear it on my back," she says, hangs up.

Dinner Table Drama

The necessity of syntax in written letters makes people think formally. None of hers are as playful as when talking at leisure. Serious, factual, formal, totally opposite the phone conversation or rambling hours of needling talk, jokes outrageous and sometimes profound, for years she has easily been able to say, "you exhaust me," the cue to retire so she can recoup. In the immediate present since husband Marvin died she has proved more talkative, can go 4 hours at a clip without exhaustion, although surely will deny it.

Today, February 12, 2003, is the day Lib and Marvin were to marry 20 years ago. It snowed so bad the wedding was postponed. Anne, Joe, Joey and Ginny on their way from West Virginia were marooned. So they got married the next day, Sunday, in the afternoon.

"All in a rush?"

"We were 72 and 75, couldn't wait."

The next day was Valentine's Day.

We are not postponing anything today however, but seek the dangerous ground. Where men and women spar and all male generalizations will be disproved.

Marvin used to object to Bea and Larry's dinner table drama. Bea would make any statement and Larry would contradict. She would become emphatic. He would raise his voice. She would back off and acquiesce. Elizabeth never noticed the drama till Marvin pointed it out, A needling B into being dictatorial.

"Have you ever done this herself?"

"*I don't know!*"

Relationships

She's big on relationships, will say to me that if my 17 year old son isn't as confident as I'd like it's my fault, then adds, "I don't blame you."

She's getting soft.

It won't last.

They say you can tell a lot from the eyes. Her father Howard had light brown, her mother Anna, dark brown, Henry Mack hazel, her brother, grey, sister-in-law Bea, medium brown. Sister Flo, dark brown. No wonder I had a hard time with them. For herself she equivocates she's got "eye-colored eyes," any color that shows up, yes, as long as it's blue and green and denied as simultaneously as the Russian émigré.

When I say goodbye I say, I love you.
She says it right back.
Years ago such words met an unbridled cynicism.
It will again.

When she had "institutionalized" herself, as she put it, these "remarks" went to a whole new level. Harping on her death so much she drove her niece and daughter to tears. Remarks to me, "a lot of tissues were used." She does the same to nephew Robert. His son asks what she loved the most in life. She coruscates, "relationships." Ha. Like the crustacean on the rocks! The inveterate loner always admitted it. Won't have anybody live with her. When you visit you stay in the motel. Relationships! One sided ones. Relationships. Family. Ask around. Her brother used to call her every night before she married. At 72. Every night! Then once a week.

What she really liked was travel, #2 on that day's list.

Basement

At 93 she doesn't exactly agree there's something just around the corner as her mother did, but if there were she'd be too busy to contemplate it. From the basement file cabinet the executrix has pulled a flat plastic cake box from the bottom drawer. Now it's on the table, filled with Indian head pennies in poor condition. She is putting them up into penny sleeves. Some of them are still wrapped in foil. There are buffalo head nickels too and some quarters, but not the full silver. Marvin was laying up stores.

"Marvin kept a few things."

With just this one example she pokes back into the dusty bin of yesteryears again, with a hearty hi-ho silver, comes up with some perspective.

As to the American Revolution: if you could risk your life for your country you could go to the balls in 1777. They had a big one for the officers after the Battle of Skippack, some Mennonites observed.

Switching to the Mennonite hat, "what's the reason for the hat?

So you can't see the hair? Short pants, long pants. If at 16 they put up their hair these are generational fads.

She's read her book, been to the desk, watched TV and eaten, but missed the many appointments canceled by snow and rain. The taxes are due, the house cleaners canceled, the shopping sprees, the light bulbs, the shipments of fruit and crackers, new batteries in the smoke detector, I'm having a hard time catching up to her. At least it's not another bouquet of flowers.

"You'll get over it," I tell her.

After the fiat rejection of "Conrad Reiff and the Pennsylvania Religion" by the historical society she reminds me that the Montgomery Co. Historical Q publishes articles.

She goes to her desk and signs stock proxies! Told to save 5 years tax records, maybe she has more. Asked about long range plans by other old ladies, " I hope to nap this afternoon." Is Nonsense not a genre?

It is the pain of our growing we can't deny. You get the pain and then comes the pleasure. Liberation was always more fun than prison. The left leg has been forgiven for its inattention to detail in a life of detail. Isn't she down in the basement today going through her past on top of the dryer? Her barbs of mockery, of two sons eulogizing mother and father as sibling rivalry, stick out of my arm.

A Thousand Years

In these last days of thousand year chiliasts everywhere, post-Christian is a phrase used by her Presbyterian minister at Media, a church historian. The phrase takes us over into those realms characterized with all the other post-modern, post-Christian of *the salmon-falls, the mackerel-crowded seas.* She adds, post-coinage, as if she expects coins are not much longer for this world either. To think she would outlive the penny!

Of course I want to add post-mythological, but that would mean empirical which is experiential, thus existential and moral by choice. What's on the other side of the post-Christian age?
Barbed wire.

Before communion the post Amish Conservative Mennonites stand up in their pews and repeat the ritualistic saying that was said as far back as the 19th century, "as far as I know I am at peace with God and with my neighbor," sometimes adding that if anybody has anything against them that they should please come and tell them.

Nasty.

When I got up on this occasion I hadn't been among them six months so I got a pass, told them I hadn't know them long enough to have anything against them, which however did change, but that God had told me he loves all the contractors at the contractor's registry run by the city and also he loves all the lumpy people at Sears and in that sense anyway I could say that I loved all of them, and sat down.

The oddity of this peace business is that Jesus himself, in the flesh, was at peace with practically nobody. He chewed up all the disciples but John, excoriated the scribes and their buddies the Pharisees, only had kind words for sinners, tax collectors, sick people and lepers. Oh yes, and women! So they're at peace but he is bringing a sword.

What am I missing?

She agrees in a way that furthers the argument, returns to her favorite theme, walk a mile with a camel, or, see it as they did. Many of them swore allegiance to the King of England, but shortly thereafter their loyalty was perforce to the colonies. Only Bishop Christian Funk saw that the truth was that their much desired freedoms of worship were going to be endemically tied to the new government, not the old, and that the old (British) was a tyranny anyway.

Should we remain in Egypt because our fathers were born there, one could have asked. Like the charismatics today, "rebellion is as witchcraft," so CIA religion says submit to the authorities over you, no matter what. They were unaware of the salutary example of Henry VIII and Oliver Cromwell. Or even Dietrich Bonhoeffer's effort to immolate Hitler. Who did they think King George was anyway? Swear papers and sign to King George Leviathan right out of Hobbes majestic who lost the American colonies and went mad, governed in the most abstruse doctrines of piscine theology.

That's it really, they had no idea of politics, history or government, let alone current affairs, but made decisions anyway. All they knew was that somebody once made a promise and damned if they wouldn't keep it. As historical Mennonites working their way down the Rhine, she's proud of their lack of education.

I resist of course saying they were uneducated because every time a Mennonite became a thinker he got kicked out. They said his ego got big. The Pennsylvania freedoms stemmed solely from Penn, promises to the king were formalities. This conflict of loyalties appears even dramatically in the life of Schlatter, a Reformed pastor, who was on both sides and imprisoned in the Revolution for treason. Conflicted in several directions, against the loyalty oath, against oaths in general, and yet for the freedoms they sacrificed to attain.

She likens it to the youth in Austria, Czech Republic and Poland in the 30's before arch diabolical Germany. In the beginning kids thought it was a fun Weimar thing, trying to outwit the authorities. They never imagined it would come to a holocaust. That's what kids do, don't take trouble seriously. That's why they survive or don't. After, overcome by naiveté they are overcome by guilt. Likewise all the other betrayals, from post-Christian theologians who live in gated shelters where they escape street life, burglars and gangs. In this peaceful enclave they concoct fairy tales about the peace God, to the tune of betraying 300 years of Mennonite testimony. And all for the equivocation that "they should all be one," Socrates' spit survives, surrendering the truth is to die a greater death. She is not willing to admit to the post-Christian era, just that the days are difficult to recognize truth. Commenting on my Mennonite experiments, she kids, "you better change direction" or you'll get confused! I told her that in 1961 I proposed to the Presbyterians that they inform themselves about racism and poverty, wrote efforts to no avail. Years later they came full force as liberals into the radical fray, but it was too late because by then the battle had shifted to the environment, and by the time they had got there too late, it had shifted again, and again. Like crows on corpses. Like Noam Chomsky thinking pedo Woody Allen a great artist.

I didn't tell her that because I'm really just trying to brighten her day with a little conversation.

Clarify the difference between the radical and the liberal like a hermit crab inhabiting the shell that the rad has left behind. How many times can that shell be lived in anyway?

We close. She says my first son should be a doctor "I think he has the intellect for it." Also that he has something rarely observed in children, he knows how to cope with people. In 1992 when I brought him to the meeting to move the aged P's he entertained himself, was never in the way.

Today, she says, too many people consider themselves victims, threatens to preach, but trades it for lunch. Doesn't slam down the phone. Says to remember her to all.

Sweet old thing huh? Says the secret of competitiveness is to contain despair, anger and frustration and take it out in the game. No, not a fighter. Youngest son Andrew, picking up paper in the alley, stands in the ditch with his arm raised, eyes in the middle distance, impresario conducting spring.

Dog Joggy is older than her, about a hundred. We were walking him in the alley when a Latin immigrant, walking his own dog, let it go. The dog came bounding up while wife Pat sang out that they were going to fight, had before. I got a big stick from our alley cleaner and the dog stopped as its owner went on down the canal. He said he didn't speak English so I shouted at him, *cerrado el dogo*! It's all in knowing how to get along.

She took salesmanship but had to drop it. The premise was that if you could sell a car you could sell anything. She couldn't drive.

Work

In high school she was a member of The Inevitable Three, or the RST, as they were called, that is, Elizabeth Reiff, Dorothy Sterling (Dot) and Rose Taylor. The Inevitable Three, always together, were all good students who were not in with the "playgirl" crowd, the smokers, the make-ups. Dot and Rose went to Philadelphia Normal School, a two year course to become elementary school teachers, though Dot went to Temple and Penn State and eventually got a degree. She first taught manual training (!) then became a school counselor. Rose worked with a Mr. Wurtz, who had society connections, doing "genealogy." Of course Libby did genealogy of a sort too, certificates into which she calligraphed the name and the date of one of the Daughters of the Magna Carta according to the required font, usually Old English. A buck each. Can you see the Dutch radical scribing for the Chestnut Hill rich? Well, at the time she was 20. As she says, the 8th graders of today are far more knowledgeable about the world than high school grads were in her day. In another era she'd have been with the French underground. As it is her resistance is against time and entropy. She doesn't think about the struggle on purpose, stands alone against all the forces of decay, "the wrackful siege of battering days." Shakespeare wrote it for her, his sonnet, me too, "that in black ink my love shall still shine bright." She says that out of her high school class of 375 they never had one reunion.

In art school on different days they would take different trips. One she remembers is the trip to the reconstruction of Chalkley Hall, the American Engineer's Building in Frankfort. This watercolor is extant. They hand measured every part of the building so that the pieces were all done to scale. These measurements were first set down in a notebook.

She received her diploma in 1930 and took some contract work, painting oil murals for instance on a restaurant, The English Garden, on Chestnut Street in downtown Philadelphia, hollyhocks and brilliant garden scenes above the wainscot. All the painting at art school had been in watercolor, but when she told her employer this he said that if you can paint watercolor you can paint anything.

She was hired by Strawbridge's at $18 a month and having an art degree was put in the fabric department as an extra. You can see the logic. She was a big girl, they thought, could handle the 50 yard bolts of cloth. Such things then, odd jobs, free lance art, Strawbridge's, odd painting, drawing genealogy certificates occupied her until 1934 when she began to work for a Merrill Krauthammer in Souderton, Ephrata and West Chester. His idea was to innovate retailing in a new type of Woolworth store where all merchandise was on full display, especially the better things. Being ahead of his time he was undercapitalized. She ran the store in Souderton 1934-5 and in Ephrata in 1936. In 1937 with the recession humming, she was making $20 a week.

In 1939 she began work for Snowdens, a department store in Media, commuted from her home in Philadelphia, staying there the whole week during the busy season, Christmas, and, as I incessantly teased her as a teenager, second Christmas, Mother's Day. For 5 years she commuted thus, moved permanently to Media in 1944. During the commute she would lose herself in books from the lending library at the store, one mystery each way. On the earlier trips to Souderton she nearly failed to get off some Sunday nights at 9 PM, preoccupied with, for example, *40 days of Musa Dheh.*

Her first job had been at the Mennonite Vacation Bible School where she was hired as a helper for $8 a week. There was no air conditioning. So her father said to her, "you get an allowance, you don't need that money, the church can hardly afford it. You should think about not accepting it." Her allowance was $2 a week. She turned the salary down. The words speak for themselves. Without inferences how do you make judgments?

We talk more about books and art. Eden as gardener, soap maker, potter, Aeyrie as photographer. Of Nathan Englander's stories, Sammy Kaye and the court jester, fairy tales, the Pied Piper of Hamlin, Dr. Zhivago's remake film, Pasternak turning in his grave. That's what they used to say of their mother, that she was "whirling Annie" turning over at the world's follies.

Another recurring theme, the pathology of parenthood, what to do about the baby, whether it be Jake (feel sorry for him because he's the youngest), Howard (put upon) or another friend, "with his mother (as an adult) he acted like a child." This leads to the burning question of left-handedness. The question is whether Andrew is left-handed because he throws left and bats left, but hits tennis right, but we think his left shoulder and arm are stronger. Howard was left-handed, hence it is in Andrew's genes. Grandma was always on the lookout for lefties among her own children so she could intervene and change them over. Howard was given a rough time and couldn't initially get his business degree because he was a lefty. Lib herself is ambidextrous. Puts ribbon over the ends instead of crossing it in the middle and when she showed this way to the Christmas help at Snowden's they complained they weren't left-handed. But Lib couldn't write left-handed, but was very conscious of it because of Grandma.

Teachers

Anna knew women born in the 1880's who taught at age 18 with little certification and no real credentials. Libby notes that her mother remembered Henry's students made fun of his Rhadamanthine beard with its chestnut undertones, called him "half-breed," so he taught at least till Anna's girlhood. Henry had enrolled for several terms at Mt. Pleasant Seminary in Boyertown that year, 1875, also the home of Elisabeth Bechtel whom he would marry. He went to Reading in October that year to attend a teacher's institute. One of the texts he bought was "Methods to Teach Reading," and by December he already must have been a teacher for he bought "20 oranges (for scholars)" and on 31 Jan 1876, "one glass for schoolhouse." His father had been a teacher too and also his brother Peter was licensed by the Lutheran Synod of East Pennsylvania in Harrisburg for ten years. Jesse Mack, Henry's son, the artist who died in his 20s, had red hair. Why there should be prejudice against red hair mocked is an atavism not so well hidden today among geneticists who want to clone a Neanderthal baby to make a super soldier, red hair or not.

Anna whose vision for education was "optimism helps motivation." finished 6th grade but her daughter graduated #5 in a class of 375 because she flunked gym, otherwise her place would have been 2 or 3. In another era she'd have been at Harvard. For somebody whose every move today is deliberate it seems surprising she could have flunked gym. Eighty girls and Miss Wurt, an unmarried teacher of females, but it was a nasty teacher, made them hang on to the end of a rope and vault over the horse, which she flunked. She flunked horse.

She flunked car too. Her brother in a mood of societal improvement was teaching her to drive when she ran into a tree. That tree yet stands as well. So she couldn't go to Normal School because of the 7 credits of gym. She was too proud to get a principal's exemption certificate. Another surprise.

The social studies teacher, Miss Franklin said, "Miss Reiff you don't have any initiative" because she wouldn't talk in class, but she didn't want to. Outies never understand Innies. Where could you find a person with deeper purpose and strength of character, greater initiative, but only to achieve what she herself had chosen? Which raises the interior vs. exterior laurels and brings into question the

Rimbaud analogy as to which is greater, the end in the beginning or the beginning in the end. Surely the reader can solve it.

I sent wife and oldest son to visit her because she had said she wanted for feminine company. I wrangled tickets to the old Barnes Museum at the last minute and they got her into a wheelchair and into the Barnes where the native artist had never been, every inch of its walls covered with Impressionist paintings. She wants to be cajoled I guess into things that must be buried deep down that is turned away from. I'd like to take her to concerts, a play, but after the gall bladder operation says she will not leave the building. Our little wifey says: "She could be President without dominating,"

Forgiveness in Faith

My grandmother and aunts were feminists. The three of them were a powerful force, my aunts toward a vision of beauty I'd not otherwise had, my grandmother Anna, a white Olympus.

They had fought mentally against domination all their lives and were nothing if not strong minded. Anna especially had reason to resist the ties, for she had had trials, first the farm, then the near loss of her first daughter, then the loss of her husband, borderline poverty and the difficulties of a father-in-law. In the midst of all this she struck an original path in folk art and religion. For Anna the issues were freedom to create and freedom to be what she chose. It is possible to understand that certain pressures might be brought to bear on a girl surrounded by religious figures.

The greatest obstacle was her stepmother, a classic case of farmer's wife. Her father Henry at this time still probably shell shocked from the loss of his first love Elisabeth, his three small children added to by two more, he was stuck on the farm. In these times he may have been just as inwardly desperate as Anna. But both had a long way to go. For Henry, the next best part of his life, after the loss of his Elisabeth, would come maybe after his second wife died and he moved in with Anna and her Elizabeth for eight years at the end of his life, a three peas in a pod of people born June 19, 20 and 21. For Anna the time came sooner. When she was 21, in 1901, she left the farm and became a tailor in the city. "It was **Anna who for sixty years painted word pictures** for her daughter about her childhood, girlhood, adult life, who expounded on marriage, child rearing, family life, who at ninety, with a terminal illness, said, 'I just can't believe I'm so old! I don't feel old.'" (2)

Best Foot Forward

We can't pass over the farm years of Annie Mack the barefoot girl and are helped to an account by a folk memoir written by daughter Anna Elizabeth in 1982, "Best Foot Forward." She presented it to me patchwork, years before she ever showed me anything else, such as Henry Mack's Ledger, and said I should rewrite it. That was impossible, but the facts in it are good, based on Anna's countless retellings of everything, including that farm domination. The farm implicates the Old Mennonite way, although not necessarily so. Both wore a negative face in *die mem*, a stepmother who had none of the light and air of Bechtels or Macks. Uncomfortable with English, with strong opinions about custom, right and wrong to enforce on the only person she could, her step daughter in this territory, no encouraging words were spoken to "Annie," like "your hair is pretty," or "you look nice in that dress." Necessity demanded she communicate her house hold skills to Anna, while Henry, diplomat and judge, sole arbiter of disputes, gave a little here and a little there. The most celebrated case was the dress Anna had made that *die mem* felt not plain enough. "Anna's father was called to arbitrate loud discussion over Annie's worldly notions as demonstrated by her fancy dress." Henry's decision, saving the appearances, was that she could wear it, but not to church.

Habermann's Prayer

There were a lot of old books left in that attic that keep telling tales. A dual language German-English translation of *Habermann's Prayers* (1873) is initialed in pencil on the second front free endpaper, "AM," that is, Anna Mack. If we assume the inscribed date of another book found there, *Christian Spiritual Conversation* (1897), as the time Anna also was reading these *Prayers*, that is, the year she joined the church, and note that one page is especially dog eared (103), that would make Anna 17. On this dog eared page, "prayer of a child," we see a girl beset with difficulty, wrestling with her stepmother, trying to subdue herself to the good:

"Give me an obedient heart that I many patiently obey, serve and show myself obliging and ready to do every thing which they desire, that is not contrary to the will of God, nor at variance with my soul's salvation, so that I may receive their blessing and live a long and pleasant life. Protect me against sin and evil society, so that I may not provoke and grieve my parents with hatred, sadness, unfriendliness, contempt, disobedience and stubbornness, so that I may not bring upon myself here on earth both their and thy curse...."

Her biographer daughter picks up the thread for us. "Annie had to fight her way. Her mother died when she was five. Her new mother objected to too much trimming on the dress. Too worldly. But when stepmother had a cyst removed from her back on the kitchen table on the farm by the doctor, it was Anna who assisted, participated in the whole operation."

Life always had a lot to bear for Anna. She was taken out of such school as there was at the end of 6th grade. "The terms were short, often the teacher of the two room school was a farmer who could teach only in winter and early summer when spring planting was finished and harvests not yet begun." (7) Anna milked the cows. Anna did the dishes, but "wanted to discover the world that lay outside her own narrow environment, inhabited by people who always wore beautiful clothes, lived in elegant warm homes and never milked cows, emptied chamber pots or cleaned the chimneys of kerosene lamps." Anna sounds at times like an indentured. "At an early age Anna decided that she wanted to "find people of more culture and education." Needless to say, the *schafige frau* (industrious woman) did not approve of this search for refinement.

By the time Anna was 11 two more boys had been born. "Always there was washing and ironing, water heated on a wood fire, clothes scrubbed on a board in a wooden tub, rinsed, wrung by hand and hung outdoors to freeze into strange shapes in winter or wrap around the clothes line in the March winds. Bedding and underwear were used just as they came from the line, but shirts and dresses and the long muslin petticoats must be smoothed by flatirons heated on the wood stove. Even in summer the fire had to be kept burning briskly to keep the irons hot. And the cooking! Breakfast must be substantial, the cows had been milked, the horses fed and the milk cans filled, ready to take to the creamery before Henry and the hired man came in to eat."

Retelling

While outwardly this life sounds a little rough, in its telling repeatedly over the years it got rougher, especially in the imagination of the daughter Elizabeth to whom die mem was "sour faced, narrow minded, rigid, very plain." She would naturally be indignant at any perceived mistreatment of her mother. Harbored a long time, this has more than a little to do with her rejections of the Dutch way she herself never knew. She writes:
"This picture of Pennsylvania Dutch farm life in the 1890's was probably common to many other parts of the rural United States.

There was one important difference. In New England, women were realizing the need to be educated; the woman suffrage movement was gaining ground. Among the plain people, there was only one sphere for women, '*Kinder, Kich un Karich*' – children, kitchen and church…at twelve Anna finished her formal education and the part of her life she enjoyed most."

There seems to be an important link in a chain here we should not miss, that is, that the daughter held a kind of unacknowledged grudge against the farm and peasant injustices reported by her mother. Even though they were not probably reported just so, the implications would be clear. You could not do what you wanted, you had to do what you were told. And this produced the most fiercely independent mind possible in a family of independent minds anyway. The structural implications just kept getting stronger as the details piled up:

"For the next nine years Annie spent six days of the week in a round of tasks that today would seem like mindless drudgery. First the cows must be milked, and this Annie hated. Getting out of a warm bed and dressing in an unheated room in the dark was bad enough, but going to the barn and sitting on a milking stool was even worse. Worst of all were the rare occasions when she dozed and the cow became restive and kicked over the milk bucket. This would bring a reprimand from her father and a tirade in Pennsylvania Dutch from her step mother."

So Elizabeth's image of the Pennsylvania Dutch gets negative, not just from the repeated details, the tirades, the drudgery, but from the language itself, which is about what Ben Franklin meant. Annie would "carry the '*zehn uhr stuck*,' [to the workers in the field], just like the modern coffee break, though often it was only a pail of cold water and some rather dry crumb cake."

The Romantic

All this and more occupied Anna outwardly, but as we know the Mennonites juxtapose the outward and the inward, as does practically everybody. Inwardly, Anna was an incurable optimist and a romantic. Later in life she deeply regretted not getting an engagement ring, but when her suitor, would be husband, skidded his horse to a stop at her door she was thrilled. At the time of which we are speaking, "one summer, Annie carried a pail of milk to a neighboring farm every day. Barefooted, as befitted a teen age girl, she was always ashamed lest a prince in disguise, riding past on a white horse should see her without shoes." The admission of the factual-realist-phenomenologist, would-be physician, non folk artist daughter is just as telling: "It never occurred to me to ask my mother where she had heard about princes on white horses, but it was probably a story remembered from one of the precious school readers.' Certainly romanticism is hard to understand.

Leaving the Farm

The rough manuscript gives many other details of farm life, foods, going to the plain church, "no organ or piano, no decoration of any kind," the plain wooden benches, long visits after church, the abbreviated social life, but anyway at age 21 you were free. So in the summer of 1901 when Anna inherited some money from her grandmother Mary Longacre Bechtel she moved to Philadelphia to apprentice herself to a tailor. "Anna and several other girls were taught women's clothing construction…there were no zippers, no miracle fabrics, each seam had to be pressed, each tiny hook and eye carefully placed and sewn with small but firm stitches. The sewing machine was operated by a treadle, there probably was not even a ceiling fan in that day."

The farm did not last long after Anna left. Her stepmother was not in good health. Anna returned at some point to help out at her father's plea. By 1906 the farm had been vacated and the whole family moved to the city. Anna married 20 December of that year.

Anna and Elizabeth

Anna's family, Bechtels, Longacres, Stauffers, Macks, were pastors, teachers, hymnists, musicians, artisans and folk scholars. Elizabeth Bechtel's death much diminished these influences in the short term of Anna's life, not only in her reading and thinking. The loss of her mother echoed and echoed, substituted as it was in Anna's mind and in her daughter Elizabeth's too with the unattractive Pennsylvania Dutch traits of her step mother.

Anna's literary remains are sparse. She had few books growing up. Henry's Ledger mentions a few schoolbooks, but no fairy tales, but she was a born romantic. Aside from the catechisms above there is only an *Appletons' Third Reader*, dated Oct 28, 1889.

But birth is irresistible. Anna expressed her hunger for the life of the mind later in the books she got her daughters. Arguably they tell the story of what she thought she missed. She could not have been more proud when she complained she had lost her little girl at age two to reading, nor done any more to have fostered all imaginative delights in her. New books were added to the house, the very ones Anna never had. Their inscriptions show that at age 5, December, 1915, *Cinderella* came at Christmas. According to her daughter this may be the single most important metaphor in Anna's imagination. Also at Christmas, age 7, came *Alice's Adventures in Wonderland*, but Anna's attempts to nurture this kind of imagination in Elizabeth were thwarted by that rational mind, what she dubbed "realism."

Alice's Wonderland fell on fallow ground where William Osler would have flourished. In later years Elizabeth read autobiographies, Malamud's *The Fixer* with pleasure, liked any new translation of *The Aeneid*, Tolstoy, Dickens. But both she and her mother were satisfied they had done their part. *Wahren Christenthum* and *Die Wandelnde Seele* were bedded down in that attic waiting.

Prayer for Strength

This memoir would not exist without the import of a prayer for strength Anna gave in 1911 when the one year old Elizabeth nearly died.

Anna got plenty of practice as a nurse, and any thing she learned she was grateful for in that summer when she nursed her first daughter back from death of the "summer complaint."

"The doctor came to the house every day, but after a week the baby had not improved. Anna saw him looking into his black bag at the rows of medicine bottles as though he could not decide which one to open. She realized that the young doctor had reached the limit of his professional expertise. That night Anna prayed for strength to give up this child whom she loved so dearly. Next morning, the doctor returned with a new medicine. Slowly the baby improved though she was now thin and pale. By summer's end she was once again the plump happy child she had been. The rest of Anna's long life was a witness to the faith that came through that experience" (17-18).

The stories of people who surrender in the face of insurmountable obstacles, praying for strength to give up a child, but why did the doc come back in the morning with a cure, why does the baby recover with or without the cure? We cannot say it is luck or piety cooked up for the occasion, it's just too important. When your daughter or son is saved you don't go around mumbling. You rejoice. It doesn't do much good to cite all the children who died just to refute this one that lived. Life trumps death in every case, especially when that life is such a partisan as to be the muse of a work about herself, which in turn saw its own sacrifice, its own surrender. Surrender for surrender is a way to proceed. So the one year old also sacrificed at 30 because she loved her mother and maybe a way of life, even a level of being, more than herself. A shocking statement, everybody giving up all the time. Life surrenders to life and to death. That's the way the folk honor the living and the dead. Who cares about justice? What we care about is love.

So Anna's love reached out in surrender and her daughter was healed. Go to a bookstore people.

Dolls

Whenever you give your life in any part for someone else or something else, as you're always doing anyway after you grow up, it tends to come back. That is, you didn't do it for yourself, but that very motive may make the act transcendent, any mother knows this. All the folk know it.

So a lot of Anna's work only gets remembered because it summoned implications of other things. "Underwear, blouses, dresses, even coats when the children were small, all came from the busy hands and sewing machine of our mother," does not do justice to it. But not just children's clothes, doll clothes. But it was especially the dolls, made to give to her daughter, made to satisfy her own lost longing that made a kind of memory of her own mother.

"Anna remembered her mother as a rather large woman with beautiful auburn hair. She remembered the doll and cradle that had been a birthday or Christmas gift" (6). And that was all the memory she had of her at age 5 when her mother died.

Little of Anna's constant creations remain and they would have been unnoticed now but for the chance remark that occurred when I was trying to provoke my informant into examining her own developed intuition. She had begun to relate how she could perceive feelings at an early age, practically from birth, and offered evidence from what she called "the worst Christmas" of her life, at age 4.

Mother Anna had had but one doll, "she remembered the doll and cradle that had been a birthday or Christmas gift," but the family lived in more than a little poverty, and she never had another. "Perhaps this year she would get a doll for Christmas! But no, it was only an orange, a couple of clear toy candies and a much needed pair of shoes." Anna of course purposed to remedy this with her daughter, so Elizabeth had dozens of dolls. But at this point the "realist" interrupted her narrative to point out that as a four year old she knew that "dolls were dolls, not real children." No maternal transference for her! But Anna went to work with much purpose and ingenuity and made the kind of folk doll that would stop an auction today.

Mother Of All Dolls

Neighbor Jenny worked in Strawbridge's fur department and had access to scraps of fur. I was never told what the body of the doll was made of, but Anna and Jenny made this doll of all dolls life-size, dressed her up and sat her in a little rocker with a black velveteen coat, a hat and scarf with white fur trimming and a little white muff with two black tails; the mother of all folk dolls, worth thousands today.

But the muff and scarf were wrapped separately, to show how large the doll was. When the child opened the wrapping she mistook the muff as though it was for her and because she couldn't "get my chubby fist in that little muff!" began to wail. Do you hear the Dutch prejudice in "chubby?" Imagine competing with your own Christmas present.

But the wail induced the mother's tears and Anna too began to cry, which was the point of the story. The daughter at ninety four remembers that at four she thought that it wasn't right to make your mother cry and stopped. Anna never knew her daughter had had this epiphany, not that she was ignorant of her little Dutch prodigy. Had Elizabeth become the first female surgeon at Women's Medical Center she would no doubt have boasted that she was a peasant surgeon.

Anna not only made dozens of dolls for her daughter, she continued the practice long after. The ladies of her church made dolls to sell at their annual bazaar. In a photograph taken in 1955 in Anna's home at least 12 dolls are arrayed for "a private pre-bazaar view at the home of Mrs. Anna Reiff." The trunks in the attic also contained various forms of doll clothes in finished and unfinished states, as well as some old dolls.

Gardens

Anna was honored in 1970 at a Woman's meeting for her life long efforts at gardening and sharing her successes: "she has always had special results in whatever she was growing – whether children, African Violets for her window sills, begonias for porch boxes, or forcing hyacinths in the winter from January until Easter…she would give us leaves from her finest African Violets…one can remember the dolls she dressed and the aprons…another project was the shoulderettes – thirty of them for Presbyterian Hospital and dresses for T. M. Thomas center. She made quilts for each child and for herself. These were kept and doled out in the breakup of the house. Quilts, dolls, clothes, food, preserves, gardens outside, African violets inside in full bloom on every window sill. So often a poet cannot write what pleases the ones who matter most, those closest, but that editor that issued Elk and Aspen, wrote, "We would like to accept these poems for the 2021 spring/summer issue of FRiGG. Please say they are still available! Pleeeease. Especially "Doll Shop." We love "Doll Shop" so much."

Bonnets, Hats and Coats

Letters were an important part of Anna's life, but she did not keep them, held the notion that their purpose ceased when read and so they were disposed. No literary remains of hers, all her doings were oral, after dinner in her home, on every occasion she would talk absorbingly about the people she had known. All that remains of this, even close to verbatim, is the above biographical manuscript. Oddly she did keep the decorated postcards, a kind of early Christmas card, sent to the family in the early 1900's from other family members. Sometimes they have only an address and no writing at all. The folk think the folk are eternal, always remembered, so while she kept an old photo album of the late 1800's, none of the photographs are identified. Nor could her daughter identify any of them at the end of her day. They must be of her greater family however, so that makes them Bechtels I guess.

Elizabeth remembers hearing continually of the most important letter Anna might ever have received, from her Uncle Andrew in 1914, no doubt written in German. This narrative is omitted from BFF, except to say that "At the time Anna joined the church [1897] local custom did not require the wearing of the prayer covering and bonnet. A plain, untrimmed hat was acceptable, and the prayer covering could be put on just for Sunday worship." The bonnet vs. the hat became a sticking point as such things have always been among Mennonites.

It must be remembered how warm an attachment Anna had for her uncle Andrew and aunt "Lisbet." "For the rest of their lives Anna felt closer to this uncle and aunt that to the rest of her relatives" (6). Andrew Mack wrote to Anna in 1914 that if she came to take the yearly communion at Bally (Hereford) she must wear a bonnet.

There is a background for this kind of thing among the Mennonites. In 1909-1911 definite decisions had been made about how to dress. "At every conference session the question of the woman's covering was belabored. Fancy hats were more and more common among the younger women" (Ruth, 425). Anna, who had been attending the "new" First Mennonite in the city anyway, which was a lot closer to her home, conferred with her husband and decided not to go to Hereford.

Not to go to communion is a big statement among Old Mennonites. It is held only once a year. During the week prior Mennonite preparation for the event is more elaborate than most Protestant services, very personal, where everyone in the congregation attempts to reconcile themselves with everyone else. It is a little formulaic: "So far as I know I am at peace with everyone and everyone is with me and if not please come and tell me." Refusing the bonnet would make that vow impossible. While she loved her uncle, who was speaking for the community, she chose the hat!

Admittedly sometime between 1897 and 1914 they had changed their rule on this, but by then it was a much older point of contention over whether the bishops and congregations did rule. From Funk to Oberholtzer the change was binding. The Rules and discipline of the Franconia Conference, revised as of July, 1933 state clearly that "…Sisters shall not wear hats" and "…if they would not comply, would have to be rejected" (Wenger, 433). These rules were not enforced universally, but how could you not see whether a woman wore a hat? So the die was cast.

The influential precedent of such behavior in her grandfather Bechtel's life could not have been lost upon Anna, how he had been engrafted to fill the gap left by Clemmer's release in the Oberholtzer affair because Oberholtzer would not wear his coat, thought he had a right not to wear the plain coat (Ruth, 245), although it is not quite as simple as that. His choice became a symbol of liberty against the Mennonite high doctrine of mutual submission. Maybe Anna too thought the coat/ bonnet laws a "human commandment" (Ruth, 247). But we hear in all this insistence for personal liberty just the complaint preachers had made for 200 years about people making their own decisions in Pennsylvania. This adds poignancy to Anna's apprenticeship as a tailor after she left the Old Mennonites precisely over the issues of dress that caused the Mennonite division of 1848. In the end Anna decided for subsequent generations not to be what she was, whether farmer, plebian or Mennonite, and forced her children into either open conflict or conformity in the war between truth and the world, why the giants had been left behind in the promised land in the first place, to prove that because the law of God is in their heart their feet do not slip. So they slipped and were rescued, slipped up, stood up.

Death of a Husband

Anna wanted to be free, so it was hard to bear constraint when her husband died, leaving her dependent on her father-in-law, Jake, for her husband Howard had a large investment in Heister and

Reiff Co. that his father owned. Jake had been a storekeeper in the world of Hereford and Clayton and Reading before 1900. One of the reasons Anna chose his son for a husband was because he was not a farmer. She was severing ties forever with that world. Father Jacob had a reputation as a sharp dealer. There were implications that he couldn't keep a location for too long. In at least one of these alleged cases he has been proved innocent.

Elizabeth's attempt to understand Jake produced the realization that his daughter-in- law didn't like him any more than he liked her, but showed it in more pleasant ways, always inviting him and his wives to family events. Secretly in their beds they all thought son Howard dominated. The party line ever since has been that Jake, as she has listed in her notes, was a "big shot, unfeeling, dominating, jealous, sharp trader, cheap skate, cigar smoker, reprobate in early life." She could have added "bad influence" since her father, like Jake, began to smoke a cigar a day at age 40! Howard's early death is attributed to his father, who either worked him to death or caused his heartburn: "in later years, Howard attributed his chronic indigestion to those hasty and interrupted meals which were a way of life when the family lived behind the store" (4). But now of course we can say it was hardening of the arteries.

A lack of freedom loomed all around them, most seriously from economic circumstances. Libby's father, Howard R., died at 46 almost without life insurance. Old Mennonites didn't believe in insurance, much the way 18th century fire companies didn't believe in putting out fires since obviously the fire was a signal from above identifying evildoers. The fire company was there to protect the neighbors, hose down their properties, separating the just from the unjust but Howard R. did take out a life insurance policy just in time after his first two children were born, a $7000 policy on the quiet.

Anna had chosen Howard chiefly on the basis that he had left the proletariat on the way to business school, just as, at the same time, her mother left the farm and sought him as a husband. Elizabeth's brother graduated Penn State and went up the executive beanstalk. Her maverick sister wrote limericks and the first text for minority slow learners. But Elizabeth studied art and longed to be a doctor. So they all escaped the farm, even if business was equally stultifying.

Inferences have been made and reports of memories given. She knew the mind of her father who died at 46. She could talk to him, was proud that he could add columns with both hands while talking on two different phones, and that he sent left-handed postcards. She hugely understates the pain of his loss when she was 17. He was a vigorous looking man, somebody other men took seriously, piercing eyes, but he was just sitting down to read his own philosophy under the palm at the end of the mind when he was stricken.

Old Jake

If you offer a sympathetic ear and a disembodied presence, as I do by phone, you eventually wish you had the power to forgive sins, for it is much like a confessional. She's been thinking that she shouldn't have hated grandfather Jake, even though he had a domineering disposition, wanted to be in control. He was youngest, she says, and the youngest often feel like they "don't quite make the grade."

Widowerhood had taken Jake as well as Henry Mack, except that it kept on taking Jake. From Jake's point of view when he got married at 21 everything was rosy. He had a son, but his wife got TB and died. He remarried and his second son died, followed later by the death of that wife. He remarried a third time and again an infant son died. Out of this remark comes Elizabeth's realization for the first time that what Jake said to his grandson Howard about his mother remarrying when her Howard had died was only a replay of the expectations of his own life. He'd lost his wife and he remarried, not too extraordinary that he'd think Anna would too. This understanding is way too late.

Of course she admits her mother Anna was independent, had all along wanted time without Howard's father present, although she invited him to all the family dinners with all the others: (maternal) Grandfather Henry, stepmother Sarah Ann, Jacob L., and wife Willomena. The two middle of these people were not Anna's favorites.

Jacob L. bought his son Howard a car in 1917, a Buick 7 passenger touring car, with stick-on curtains that hung on pegs. The proviso was that Howard would drive Jake. On these excursions men rode shotgun and spit out the window. Now you see why I walked on tiptoe around these ladies, they had legitimate grievances. Boorish behavior at best. Jake sat in the front while Anna and the children, or Wilhelmina, Jake's second wife, sat in the back. Jake would light a cigar but not smoke it. He chewed it.

She says that Jake couldn't grasp his first and only surviving son's sudden death in 1927. Filled with grief he wanted to "kick the cat," i.e., lash out in grief at something or someone. That turned out to be Anna, she feels. Jake went a little wild in his fantasies, thought he was going to have his grandson Howard run his business. Instead his grandson gave him the business, but I'm wondering how in the world I'm going to pay for all this insight at the current rates:

"It was the time and the place of his saying [Anna would remarry] that angered Howard. When I needed money (at the College of Design) I went to see Jake [and hated it, she doesn't say].

He would show me some of the things he had, he gave me some old pottery."

You notice though that she's not giving the old pottery away, at least not yet. Then suddenly, ironically, she commits herself to that old institution of life, the hospital rest home, and gives it all up at once, in toto, except for a chair, a bookcase and a testament of acceptance. I expect Billy Budd to come leaping out. Mennonites either fight to the death or give up the ghost.

I Cried With Her

Anna reverted again to the girl on the farm solving problems at the demise of the accused misanthrope diabetic Jacob L. in 1929, brought the bed down the stairs, wept with the wife at his condition, did the dirty work in a pinch:

"He sat in the rocker with his foot on the table and he had sat there all day unable to move, suffering agony with that leg, sleeping most of the time from dope which the doctor gave to relieve him, moaning with pain as soon as he was awake. Grandma cried and for a bit I cried with her as the enormity of the situation dawned upon me. I tell you I never missed Dad more, so I pulled off my coat and hat and decided to stay till we got him to bed, but alas, he could not get upstairs, so I and the housekeeper took the bed apart and brought it down. We even had to pull him into the front room in his rocker till we put up the bed."

No examples of Jake's dominance of his son are given, unless it's the interruptions at dinner, it is just assumed, like her question of Jake's second wife, Wilhelmina, "how did she cope with her husband's domineering nature?" (5) along with the anecdote that she died of pneumonia after scrubbing the cellar floor on her knees in winter. These read like caricatures, like one of Faulkner's characters, "her life had been worn out by the crass violence of an underbred outlander" (*Knight's Gambit*, 6). If Jake had tried a palace coup he would have found the army, navy and air force against him.

She interprets inferential evidence of grandfather Jake from photographs: "he is serious, with his full lower lip thrust out aggressively, and rimmed with a scraggly beard." But she also admits, "my personal memories from childhood and early youth are colored by my mother's stories and analysis of his character in later years." Her mother had been much offended by the masculine in the form of four high spirited brothers of her childhood. In adulthood the daughter remembers, contra manhood, that her uncle was crude, her father was dominated and her grandfather was worse.

Forgiveness in Faith

At the end of his life, my old dad, grandson Howard, had told the story of Jake's peccadillo so often I knew it well. I always listened for slight changes, nuances of expression. One evening in 1993, the first time I took the trip to Philadelphia with son Aeyrie, then seven, all light and joy, he told it for the last time. The day after his father had died he and his grandfather were in the garage. Jake was just leaving, but turned at the last moment and said, "don't worry, your mother will be remarried soon." The nineteen year old ordered him off the property!

At the time of this last retelling we were standing in the middle bedroom looking at Jake and Kate's framed wedding certificate. Dad was 85, his voice was raised and he was sputtering a little. I put my arm around his shoulders. "Dad, what do you say you forgive this man? Can you do that? Can you forgive him in faith?"

"Yes."

Works Cited

Alice's Adventures in Wonderland and Through the Looking-Glass. "To Elizabeth / From Mother / Dec. 25, 1917."

Christian Spiritual Conversation...with an Appendix. Lancaster: John Baer's Sons, 1892.

Cinderella; or, The Little Glass Slipper. And other Stories. NY: A.L. Burt. "Dec. 1915. Elizabeth Reiff."

William Faulkner. *Knight's Gambit.* London: Chatto & Windus. 1951

MORNING AND EVENING / PRAYERS / FOR EVERYDAY OF THE WEEK/BY / /DR JOHN HABERMANN. Philadelphia: IG. Kohler, 1873.

Gerhard Roosen. *Christliches Gemuths-Gesprach.* Lancaster: John Baer's Sons, 1869.

John L. Ruth. *Maintaining the Right Fellowship.* Scottdale, PA: Herald Press, 1984.

J. C. Wenger. *History of the Mennonites of the Franconia Conference.* Telford, PA: Franconia Mennonite Historical Society, 1937. Republished by Mennonite Publishing House. Scottdale, PA, 1985.

Elizabeth Young. Best Foot Forward. Manuscript biography of Anna. Winter, 1982.

Three Mack Brothers

Henry Mack

Henry Mack (1854-1946) lived longest of the Mack brothers. His wedding with Elisabeth Bechtel joined two illustrious families of Mennonite families and ministers. While it is possible to see outwardly the effects of suffering it is not easy to judge their inward results. He of course is the grandfather of our Libby and the father of Anna Mack.

Courtship

His Ledgers (1875-1900) in a clear and flowing hand, give a detailed window on folk life and the communities of Clayton and Douglas of 1880 and 1890. They poignantly relate his courtship, marriage and bereavement of Elisabeth Bechtel.

She is addressed endearingly immediately he begins that ledger in 1875. First she is Lizzie, then she is L. L. B., her initials as embroidered also on a show towel linen, Lizzie Longacre Bechtel. We know when he buys her a handkerchief or an orange or visiting cards or takes her out for strawberries and peanuts, April 10, 1875, and after: "Fare to Boyertown (went to see Lizzie)." "Lizzie and I went to Franconia," "L. L. B. & myself went to celebration to Hill Church. Spent for watermelons, etc. - .25." By the end of 1875 he had taken more than thirty round trips, most by train, between Allentown and Millerstown, from Boyertown to Barto, from Pennsburg to Collegeville.

Elisabeth lived in Boyertown, site of the Mt. Pleasant Seminary that Henry enrolled in for several terms that year. Clearly suited to being a teacher, he went to Reading in October to attend a teacher's institute. One of the texts he bought was "Methods to Teach Reading," and by December he already must have been a teacher for he bought "20 oranges (for scholars)" and on 31 Jan 1876, "one glass for schoolhouse."

Henry was a musician and played the violin. Twice he bought an E string for it. He joined a baseball club in 1875, enrolled in Mt. Pleasant Seminary, commuted weekends between Millersville and Allentown to business college, went frequently to Boyertown, where, again, both Lizzie and the seminary were located. For these activities he continually buys paper collars and cuffs, has his hair cut and boots mended.

He has a sweet tooth, buys cakes, oranges, peanuts, "sassfril," gumdrops, "sparking candy," soda water, pineapple syrup, peaches, watermelon, mint sticks, pretzels. On 19 June 1875 he has "one tooth extracted" and immediately notes, "bot candy." Again 3/21/76, "one tooth extracted." On March 28 he buys "four artificial teeth."

Teacher

In the first year of the ledger Henry did much business with writing and visiting. He writes a steady, neat hand, easy to read, with delicate flourishes. Even his shorthand is legible. He buys paper, envelopes, cards, several bottles of ink, including carmine, more stationary and envelopes, scroll cards, stamps, visiting cards, postcards, copy books, a daybook, ledgers, account books, steel pens, penholders, lead pencils.

In April, 1875, following a four day course at the Mt. Pleasant Seminary in Boyertown, he enrolled in the Allentown Business college where he "paid for the full course…" stationary and board, by borrowing $106 from relatives, Lizzie Mack, Grandmother Stauffer, Mother, Lizzie S. Mack (his sister), Andrew S. Mack and Jesse Mack. He paid the tuition monthly and gave promissory notes to his family which were then repaid. During this period he accounts for his trips from home on a frequent basis, point of departure Millerstown, to Allentown, as if he came home roughly every other weekend. These trips began on April 17 and ended about August, as does the repayment of most of the money he borrowed, so it seems he was through the course by September.

In October he went to Reading to attend a Teacher's Institute and immediately began teaching, for he notes on 3/28/1876 that he "Rec'd fr Treasury Washington District for 5 mos teaching @ $30 per mo $150." The last day was Mar 17, "candy and cake for scholars last day."

His income for this first year was $174.62; $150 of it came from teaching and the next largest source of income was for his labor, for which the going rate seems to have been about a dollar a day. He receives $5 from Joseph Moyer for labor and in all $21, including a dollar received from J. Gabel to "drive cow to Gabelsville."

In 1876, December 25, all this culminates, full of gaiety, "presented to my Darling for a Christmas present - $5.00. Later that winter, "paid for sleigh, to take a ride to L. L. B." He records birthday presents, Christmas presents, Valentines. Then Feb. 25, 1878 "1 Pr. Calfskin boots (wedding boots)," and March 9, "wedding trip to Franconia."

After marriage Henry moved from his father's farm in Clayton, Berks County to a rented farm in Douglas, Montgomery County, not that he ever loved farming. In 1880, their first child, Annie is born, "March 18, 8 yds. calico (Dress for my darling)" and we know it must be a maternity dress for the daughter is to be born June 21st 1880, the day after his own birthday in fact! Now he has to buy (June 15) a "German Family Bible," which still exists with the names and dates written in his hand, and a "high chair for Annie" (Nov. 3), a "doll baby for Annie" (Dec. 23, 1884), and a "book for Annie" (Jan. 30). It seems at this juncture that she is to be his much loved little daughter. On May 21, 1883, comes the birth of "Willie,' his first son, and the entry, "blocks for children" (Nov. 13, 1884).

Lots more can be said of Henry, how he becomes the guardian of his brother Peter's children after his death in October 1879, of his time as a schoolteacher, his almsgiving, his purchase of a tombstone for brother Peter (Aug. 6, 1881), his interactions with the community, working for his brother Andrew, hiring laborers, that is, neighbors for the harvest.

Bereavement

You know it's coming as you read the Ledger and dread it the more because he doesn't know. You see him getting busier and busier, first a daughter, then a son born. His accounts grow. He's not as indulgent. The sassafrases are replaced by farm implements, the sometimes blue ink is black and a new pen is firmer of hand. A lot more business is conducted, butter and egg especially. "Sundries for wife," he writes, "Christmas present for wife," as if he likes the word, a "pair of shoes, medicine for wife."

But the ledger stops suddenly on March 31, 1885.

The most informative entries have been in the pages and pages of Expenses, but in the two volumes that go forward from 1876 to 1898 only blank pages occur after Lizzie had died of typhoid fever 15 days after the birth of their third child Jesse, April 7, 1885. Weakened from childbirth she did not pass the crisis of the fever, leaving this distraught husband and three very small children, Anna, Will and baby Jesse.

No crops were planted in the spring of that year. There was no harvest; no ledger was kept either. Henry gave up the rented farm. Anna and Will went to Uncle Andrew. The baby, Jesse, went to the Bechtels. You can see the devastation in the white space. Skip a couple of pages, then appears an income statement, eggs and poultry, then blank pages again, the 1886 Statement of Affairs, then blank pages The Expenses only begin again a year later on April 7.

The loss of the love of his life forces us to forgive Henry's fastidiousness, for celebrating, as he does at its outset, the Ledger's reason for being: "I, H. S. Mack, being this 24th day of March, in the year of our Lord 1875, free, I start business on my own condition." We see the expense and the tragic cost written large in the absence of his wife on those later pages.

But it's not only in its absence of accounts that his grief appears. Exterior to the ledger we learn that he underwent an affliction similar to his brother Andrew, but what this consisted of besides depression, loneliness and despair we do not say, except it passed after a year or so. In these circumstances he stands undone for all to see, absent from the reason of his being. His rigorous purge gains our sympathy. Henry Mack willingly grew attached. He lost the love of his life, suffered dissolution and heartbreak without her. He was more suited to be a teacher or a judge than a farmer.

Andrew Mack says in a letter of May 13, 1885, "We have troublesome, sorrowful times. My wife is at my brother Henry's for two weeks by Sunday. He feels very lonely and sad so that sometimes he cannot be comforted." Following her death Henry "hired a housekeeper to look after the children and run the house, but he was unable to cope with all the problems." Finally he gave up his farm and went to live with relatives. His two oldest children, Anna and Jesse stayed with Uncle Andrew Mack for two years.

On recovery he remarried, during the time of a blizzard, in '88, about two and a half years after Lizzie's death. His dislike of farming made returning to it all the more difficult. He was quite thin, "looked like Abe Lincoln" his daughter Anna was told, making her promptly think he was not as good-looking as she had thought. Sometimes he came in from the fields at noon so exhausted he couldn't eat but would take only a glass of hot water. His dream was to do something, anything, beyond the farm. He was a guardian, a teacher, a musician, sold business cards. But he knew the heights and the depths.

These highly personal and emotional accounts of loss of life and love are not to be repeated. The three Mack brothers witness an integrity and honesty and openness that arouses our own sorrow.

Two Mennonite Songbooks

The editions in that attic prove by their inscriptions that Elisabeth Bechtel was literate in English. She signs her name in both German and English in the German/English New Testament, "Elisabeth S. Bechtel" and "Lizzie S. Bechtel." The John B. Bechtel family spoke both languages. Of course Henry Mack's entire ledger is in English, but Andrew Mack conducted all his writing and speaking in German. Two identical copies of the Mennonite songbook, *Die Kleine Geistliche Harfe der Kinder Zions* stand side by side in that collection, leather bound with clasps. They belonged to Henry and Elisabeth when they were courting. Hers is signed "Lizzie L. Bechtel / Feb 11th '72," his is simply stamped with his name "Henry S. Mack." Henry was "active in the Mennonite church for 60 years serving as chorister and musical director in many churches in this part of the state," he led the singing the whole of his life in these congregations (Wenger, 120). Their songbooks were kept together all the years after Elisabeth had died and they were still there in 2004.

Promise

John B. and Mary Bechtel buried five of their eight children. Of those whose birth and death dates are known, two died at Christmas, but they themselves lived into their eighties. They too had signed their names together, in the frontis of *Die Wandelnde Seel*e, fifty years before. Posthumous events are not what we imagine. How could they have believed that even with the loss of their daughter Elisabeth in 1885 they would be remembered more than a century later, and that their lives would be so sought? Folk remember.

The image of God is written in these people. The tragedies are evident, but what about the triumphs? That image fills them with all the senses of peace, a *gelassenheit* of mind from which we may learn the promise of renewal for a thousand generations, partly fulfilled now in these ten generations of the new world, and putatively, at least from the case, again and again when someone stands in your place and remembers you. What you most need to find is love and faith to believe it will be all right, because it will. Henry and Elisabeth are remembered now by a five year old who sat in the front row of an old photograph taken when Henry was 90 at Philip Mack's celebration of him. Andrew Mack, Peter Mack, John Bechtel, Anna and Mary Longacre, the Stauffers, Kate Rosenberger, all the Elizabeths are images of the beauty of God, the goodness of God, the love of God, who learned to be strong in the midst of pain and sorrow. What we say to them, they say to us. It's going to be all right. Believe in your children, in yourself, in God.

Peter Mack

Peter was a teacher and pastor who gave music lessons and operated a music store in Hummelstown in 1878, at the end of his life. From 1860 to 1870 he taught school and then was licensed by the Lutheran Synod of East Pennsylvania in Harrisburg perhaps under the influence of his wife's family. Isidore Rambo, with whom he had six children, descended from Gunnar Rambo, who emigrated from Hisingen, Sweden about 1647. He pastored a church at Watsonville before he became the pastor of Zion's Lutheran church at Hummelstown, PA for about four years. His last sermon was November 5, 1876: "preached in the morning to ordinary audience with unusual difficulty. Afternoon attended to Sunday-school duties with more satisfaction. Evening preached to good audience with more comfort." Health failing, he was forced to resign and in the spring of 1877 moved to Trappe, Montgomery county, Pa., locale of the Augustus Lutheran church first pastored by Henry Muhlenberg in 1742. and in nine months revived enough from tuberculosis that he returned to Hummelstown in the spring of 1878, and opened a music store where he taught music until the last illness that began four months previous to his death." He died at age 37. (Tribute to Rev. P. S. Mack in The Lutheran Observer).

The *Souvenir History of Zion Lutheran Church*, 1753-1893 says it was Mr. Mack's reward to witness the testimony of the Holy Ghost to his preaching in a precious religious awakening during the winter of 1874, when many who are still faithful to the consecration which they then made, gave their hearts to Christ, and the church had great joy in the Holy Ghost.

Many of the things which he suffered, in body and in spirit, during his pastorate, [spirit of travail], may never be known, either by those who caused him anguish of heart by their impenitence, or by those who rejoiced his soul by their fidelity; but the following interesting entrance in his diary on January 1, 1875, shows that, as a true shepherd, he was deeply concerned about his flock:

January 1, 1875. –Have had heaviness of heart for some weeks; partly on account of 'sins of the world,' and seeming indifference and lukewarmness of so many professed Christians; and partly from, to me, inexplicable causes. 'Cleanse thou me from secret faults,' O god. By God's help "Resolved, that 'I will leave all and follow Christ.' Resolved, That I will consecrate myself anew and unreservedly to Christ in the ministry of reconciliation. Lord, help me to this for Christ's sake, amen."

From *The Hummelstown Sun* Peter Mack, 1842-10/10/1879 37 years, 6 months, 2 days.

Now comes the work. As stated in Johann Arndt's, *Wahren Christenthem* union occurs in the beginning, but desire for perfection in the end. We have about as much control over the end as we do its beginning. The result is that self sacrifice is required.

Purgation after the heights of union and illumination seems counterintuitive. Should not illumination lead to power and control over circumstance? The premise of the Mennonite is that God is not willing to share his glory. But, they believed, God willing, to extend His will into a life to produce a work other than by human standard. This evokes humility.

Illumination could give an illusion of grandeur, so pride was the chief fear. Their favorite text says, his strength is made perfect in weakness. Purgation-produced weakness motivated the renewal of the image of God in the man, "but who ere saw, though nature can work so, / that pearl, or gold, or corn in man did grow" (John Donne, "To the Countess of Bedford," 65-66). In Arndt the pearl, gold and corn are "the image of God… raised up in you - faith, love, hope, humility, patience, the fear of God," (197) after the harrowing of the ground.

Plowing the ground is not negative if it produces such visible goods. Mennonites believed that the "crown," of trials was offered especially to bishops, martyrs, saints and Mennonites with the promise that when he has tried me I shall come forth as fine gold. These things obviously involved sickness, disease and death, as they did in the three Mack brothers, sons of Jesse Meyer Mack (1812-1892) and Susanna Stauffer (1813-1897). Andrew (1836-1917), Peter 1842-1879 and Henry (1854-1946), shared such character in common that we must give account.

Andrew Mack

Andrew S. Mack (1836-1917), as bishop of the Mennonite church from 1875 to 1917, was stricken with illness within months of his acclamation to high office. Ordained at Hereford by John B.

Bechtel on 15 Sept 1863 and elected bishop 6 November 1875, two months later he writes,11 Jan 1876:

"Since you were with us we have had many dreary hours. First, because I am not well. My sickness is in the kidneys and bladder. My nerves are also weakened. I am a little better. The doctor said if I will listen to him then I can grow well again. I am not to do any heavy physical work, not preach, not indulge in deep thoughts and not read. The latter is the most difficult for me. I couldn't keep up with reading much anyhow. Light work agrees the best and being out in fresh air. The doctor says I shouldn't preach for 2 months, but once I have my strength back I will likely begin to preach again, if the Lord would have me preach again."

In this same letter he announces that his deacon and also son-in-law John Gabel, as mentioned, has been discharged from the church for "an abominable sin." He begins, "I write tonight as I have never written before…You can't imagine how my poor heart often feels, especially at this time when I am weak and unwell," and "when I see the church and how I labored these 12 years that I served, my courage would often sink." These frank and unguarded thoughts typify his openness and honesty. It is hard not to sympathize with him in these circumstances. "I could still write much of what is on my mind, but too much writing isn't good for me either." He is hemmed in, but not so much that he condemns the fallen, "Also pray for J. Gabel. He is in great sorrow yet there are those who press him farther down…Old father Gabel was here today and he wept over his son."

He had been moved by the fall of both his elders, Gehman and Gabel. On that first occasion (1/11/71) he admonished both Mensch and himself, "that we accomplish our office faithfully." He feels the agony of adulterer Gehman's wife, "his wife thinks she can bear it with the help of God," as no doubt he feels the pain of his own daughter's betrayal.

Deep Thoughts

That he is not to engage in "deep thoughts" makes us ask, what deep thoughts were those? Deep thinking would be difficult when pressed by sickness, personal tragedy and continual bickering.

In an earlier letter of 1870 he had tried to bring harmony between brethren Detweiler and Deis. He addresses Detweiler:

"I have heard that discord has taken place between you and brother John Deis; and it came to the place where I felt that in my great weakness I should write to you…one often wishes for the best, and it will not be accepted as such, and is sometimes made worse by writing; which I hope for God's sake will not be the case with these lines…

But he doesn't send the letter, instead includes it to Mensch and adds, "I wanted to write more, but my wife thought I better leave it at that. Then I became scared to send this to them; so I thought I would send this letter to you. You may read this, then you can see a bit how my heart felt when I wrote this. Don't give this letter to brother Detweiler and Deis. Keep this letter to yourself. I am afraid they won't accept it in love."

He is weak. He is nervous. He feared rash behavior, "sometimes made worse by writing." He accepts his wife's and Mensch's counsel that the letter might endanger the situation. His technique in peacemaking is evident when he says, "when it comes to the point between you…take each other's weaknesses upon yourself."

In the next letter after his promotion, 2/27/1876 he says, "…I find myself so weak, physically and spiritually… I am still not supposed to preach, and can not work much yet." He is tested by a dispute over the building of a new meetinghouse at Boyertown. This was fallout from the Oberholtzer split of 1847 and ended up before the Pennsylvania Supreme Court. After the division in 1847 the new and old congregations had met alternately in the same building until 1876. But when the old group decided to build again they offered tenancy to the new only on the condition that they use no objectionable musical instruments.

"The new (Mennonites) wished to build with us, and we did not want that…the new (ones) wished to have a written agreement drawn up so they could show that they had their rights, but ours did not wish to commit themselves… I did not intend to be concerned with the building."

When demolition had already partly removed the old building, the New Mennonites sued for tenancy in common before the Berks County Court. This suit was denied in 1879. Subsequently the court reversed this finding. Then, upon appeal in 1883, the Supreme Court of Pennsylvania, reversed it back, finding for the Old, the occasion when John B. Bechtel had testified.

This was a truly contradictory procedure for people who did not believe in legal remedies (see Wenger, 122-23 and Ruth, 366-67) and a betrayal of the very principles John F. Funk praised in the Skippack Old Mennonites who had solved a similar situation, "they chose rather to obey the scriptural injunctions 'not to resist evil, and of him that taketh away thy goods, not to ask them again.'" Funk calls this "one of the most glorious examples of self-denial and devotion to … religious principles, presented to us in modern times" (128).

Andrew Mack always sought to prevent division. He succeeded in 1897 in the matter over whether to recognize the formation of a General Conference in the west, something the "Old" congregations distrusted.

"If the congregations in the west were in such circumstances that they needed a general Conference, he said, we are ready to let them have it, and no need fear a division or separation in fellowship from us because you vote for something that you stand so much in need of. We know that you need it and why not vote for it" (quoted in Ruth, 406). An almost unanimous vote followed in favor.

On March 12, 1876 he writes, "I will likely still be lacking in strength at times, as well as by preaching, but I must remember that whom the Lord loves He reproves, and it will likely serve for the best. Although there are still times when I feel depressed that I can't see to my office and normal business better…I have already thought that I have burdened you too much through writing. I beg patience with me in my great weakness."

His letters evidence constant concerns about seeing to his office: "we have such a serious office enjoined upon us, and I find myself so poor in accomplishing it, as it should be" (8/15/79). He is scheduling appointments with visiting dignitaries, conducting funerals, visiting the sick, including both his brothers (below) and presiding over the contentious meetings of the Conference while at the same time being a farmer.

He sticks to it too. Over a year and a half later he is still striving for unity for Detweiler and Deis, his thoughts rambling from his weakness and effort. After six years he is still working on reinstating John L. Gehman following his confession of adultery (1/11/71):

He writes, "further, dear brother, and fellow laborer in the Lord's vineyard, what shall I write to you in my great weakness and imperfection? Should I write only from the holy Scriptures? My thoughts ramble on; it is more familiar to you than me. Since I read the letter which you wrote to Gehman and what was the incident with brother Gotwals and then again between the brethren Detweiler and Deis, thinking how they are in disunity; but I still had this hope that they would perhaps stand in unity with each other again" (9/3/1877)

His loses his brother Peter to sickness (1842-10/10/1879), Lutheran pastor at Hummelstown, as his own sickness ends. "Further, my brother in Hummelstown is quite sick. I was with him last Saturday through Monday and visited him. When I left him I didn't expect him to live so long" (8/15/79). Notable similarities occur among the brothers' attitudes toward their work and toward God, especially the spirit of resignation, weakness and enforced retirement, deep humility and unwavering faith borne with grace. (Tribute to Rev. P. S. Mack in The Lutheran Observer) His "private diary contains many allusions to his bodily sufferings" (Souvenir History of Zion Lutheran Church, 1753-1893). Efforts to locate this diary continue.

By 12/8/1879, even though he is completely restored, "we are quite healthy physically, but spiritually we are weak," he is still thinking about the fallen. Of dissension and lapses of all kinds he says that "many things would not make their appearance and many difficult tasks would not need to be done and many dark clouds would not appear over us. But sin has twisted all this around and sin has penetrated through to all mankind because they had all sinned."

Sometimes his mediations involve a more visionary sort of compassion. Not only upon destinies and fates, but upon the effects of the "fire of love" in families and communities.

"It is truly as the prophet had already said, a bruised reed shall He not break and the smoking flax shall He not quench. He will not break the repentant sinner. He, namely Jesus, wants us to repent, then He will accept us, even though our faith is weak and only like a spark. So, He will not quench it, but rather ignite it. I am come to send fire on the earth and what will I, if it be already kindled? Yes, if only the fire of love in all our hearts were truly ignited that we could all walk together in love."

It sounds a lot like the *Martyr's Mirror* when he says that "if everything went well we would possibly grow forgetful of what is the most necessary, but our sorrow of which Paul writes doesn't cease." He embraces sufferers of all kinds in his letters: for "often we plan something and the loving God thinks differently. But the Lord's ways are right and good although we often don't understand it. If we love God, we know that God does all things for the best, even when we must go through sorrow here in this earthly life. But we have the promise that sorrow brings forth the peaceable fruit. So we want to walk in the ways of the Lord, that we can enter heaven and we don't wish to miss Jesus' call or be left behind" (1/25/86).

10/9/92 "So Dear brother, I will ask you a question. Can man prepare his own garment of righteousness or not?"

The reading and deep thoughts he had referred to earlier are mentioned by his niece Anna Mack, Henry's daughter, who lived with her uncle in 1886 and 1887 after her mother had died. She remembers that it was Andrew Mack's habit that "each day, after the noon meal, he would retire to the room where he had a roll-top desk, get out his Bible to study and read for an hour before he went back to the farm work" (6).

Nearly every letter of Bishop Mack inquires or reports on the health and hopes of the people around him. "Lizzie is not so well today; we hope she will soon be better. Eli's wife is also not so well so we have plenty of work and see how it will turn out" He undertakes healing efforts himself in their behalf (7/18/04):

> "Emma Rickert is already 4 weeks at home and we give her a treatment daily. We have something by which we take one of her limbs at a time and put it in, then we heat it up with a light. The limb is wrapped up and the heat is increased until the thermometer shows 300 and more, as hot as she can stand it. Then, when we take it out, it must be rubbed vigorously and the joints exercised. It takes us 3 hours daily to do this work, but it has already somewhat improved, but slowly."
>
> (4/7/98) "The old sister & widow of preacher John Bechtel is quite weak, if she is still living. So we see that one here and another there must bid us goodnight. A loving greeting in closing. A& E. Mack

Among the families that remain to a thousand generations of those who love Him who may be reading this, if in your life you have stirred compassion for others, whether you are a physician or animal lover, you can see a precedent in this man, and not be surprised that he still influences lives and hearts long after he has passed.

While his writing is personal, it is sometimes meant to be read aloud, no doubt from the pulpit as a greeting and instruction from the bishop. "Dear brethren and all who hear this read" (1/18/89).

His themes are honesty, humility and love, with a recognition of what can be done, where faith starts and work stops. Obviously these people faced death, accident, sickness and difficulty at an incidence many times our own: "we value our physical health so highly, for we value it above all earthly treasures, but when we read the Scriptures we find that a child of God must suffer much and Christ had to suffer much for our sake, for if they do these things in a green tree, what shall be done in a dry?" There two Mennonite ideas, give up your life without compromise in death and live in humility and service to others, put other's needs ahead of their own.

When Jacob Mensch, loses his wife, coincident with the last letter of Andrew Mack's in the collection, Andrew writes in sympathy and faith which would have also been his counsel to his brother Henry on the loss of his wife: "Dear brother, I regret that the sister left us… However it was Lord's will, so what shall we say? The poet says, What God has done is rightly done, His will is always fitting, whatever He has once begun, myself I'll be submitting. Yet when it comes to the point where one must give up one's dearly beloved our help, our support in difficulties and distress, and one may say, half of our lives, this causes a deep wound. But we have this comfort in the Scriptures, the one who strikes the wounds can also heal them… the words with which you have comforted others shall now be your comfort. I will say the same to you, although you have likely found that it is easier to comfort others as oneself. I must close. Writing makes me weaker. Our of love, from your weak brother, Andrew & Elizabeth Mack. Write again" (2/13/1906).

There is always an overt sense of mortality and humility. He continually refers to his weakness with several meanings, his physical incapacitation when he began as bishop, but further, his strength in weakness throughout the exercise of his office, that "strength is made perfect in weakness." He is vested with the full time care of everyone plus himself.

All of his preaching was in German and if these letters are an indication those messages were reflective and meditative. The 49 letters sample a much wider correspondence that must have taken place not only with Jacob Mensch, but with others. Years pass between letters.

It is merely accidental when a letter hits a high spot. Jacob Mensch, ordained minister of the Skippack Mennonite Church in 1867, is said to have been strong willed, par for the day perhaps, but if the two had different dispositions they were likeminded enough to travel extensively together. They were also intellectual friends: "I will be in the Schwenkfelder harvest meeting and if you could also be there we could have a discussion with each other which I would greatly enjoy before you go on your journey." Mack's sincerity and courtesy served him well in this friendship.

His continual injunctions to Mensch reflect that both are "laborers together in the Lord's vineyard." A metaphor, not of the shepherd, but of the gardener is fitting since he was himself a farmer and knew the effects of a pruned vine. The metaphor directly relates to Mack's lifelong difficulties and trials out of which, as he might say, "the peaceable fruit of righteousness" came.

There are many scriptural citations in the letters, often of familiar texts, recognizable when read aloud. Together these show an imagination thoroughly imbued with the defenseless way. Together they show the depth of vintage produced in this vineyard. *I will seek to totally surrender myself to my dear Jesus and as He decides for me is right.*

Works Cited

John Arndt. *Wahren Christenthum.* Translated by Anthony William Boehm. London, 1712. Edited by Calvin Chaddock. Boston: Lincoln & Edmonds, 1809.

Werner Heisenberg. *The Physical Principles of the Quantum Theory*. Chicago: The University of Chicago Press, 1930.

Rufus Jones, preface to Stoudt's translation of Boehme.

The Journals of Henry Melchior Muhlenberg. Translated by Theodore G. Tappert and John W. Doberstein. Reprint of Fortress Press,1942 by Picton Press, Camden, ME.

Schlabach, Theron F. "Humility." Canadian Mennonite Encyclopedia Online. 1989. Mennonite Historical Society of Canada.

Wahren Christenthem (Four Books Concerning True Christianity), Sechs Bucher vom Wahren Christentum...Nebst DessenParadiesgartliein. (Philadelphia: Georg W. Mentz und Sohn, 1832.)

Richard E. Wentz. *Pennsylvania Dutch Folk Spirituality*. New York: Paulist Press, 1993.

Die Kleine Geistliche Harfe der Kinder Zions (Lancaster, 1870).

John F. Funk. *The Mennonite Church and Her Accusers*. Elkhart, Indiana: Mennonite Publishing Company.1878.

German and English New Testament. (New York: American Bible Society, 1870). The Ledgers of Henry Mack. Unpublished manuscript books.

The Letters of Andrew Mack from the Jacob B. Mensch Letter Collection in the Mennonite Heritage Center, translated by Isaac R. Horst.

Catechism of a Martyr

"You know the trouble with Mennonites? They've always wanted to be Jews."
-- Rudy Wiebe, *The Blue Mountains of China*

Pacifists

Elizabeth's husband Marvin was a pacifist. This came up soon after he and Elizabeth married when he heard a noise in the upstairs hall of their home, just outside the bedroom door of the 80 year old scout. As the intruder began to enter Marvin slammed the door really hard into his head. End of intrusion. So I asked, what is pacifism? He said he was sorry he did it. That's like the trick questions they're supposed to ask conscientious objectors at draft boards. What would you do if somebody were attacking your home? The best answer is like his. If I hurt him I regret it.

Although early Mennonites were pretty good at escaping prison, they were supposed to be harmless, defenseless, not heroic. Their holy book, *The Bloody Theatre or Martyr's Mirror* (1660), has Mennonites still asking today, not how to put up with your anger at oppression, but "could you forfeit your life," and "what happens to you if you don't have to forfeit your life?"

It sounds like a terrible inversion to produce a book of tortures as inspiration for a people destined to live in centuries of peace. In raising the question thus we bypass common aspects of Mennonite identity, plain dress, church discipline, separation from the world, for this ideal of self sacrifice.

The Bloody Theatre is the psychological opposite of Aristotle's tragedy that should arouse and purge feelings of pity and fear. In Athens the populace was supposed to leave the theatre pacified, willing to accept and repeat contradiction, making the politician safe. In Pennsylvania the Mennonite was asked in the German translation of the Dutch whether he could leave his "flesh on the posts" of the "strait gates" as if it were some sun dance. (*Bloody Theatre*, 6).

Lapses

Temptations of the flesh, pride, shame and greed and the seven deadly sins were after the Mennonites in America. It's hard to appreciate how desperate the 19th century rural case was, with deacons committing adultery at the age of 50 and more hideous sins unnamed. It you commit adultery with a woman down the road she doesn't just move away. Everybody knows her and you. You might see her the rest of your life. Two of the earliest letters of Bishop Andrew Mack to Jacob Mensch relate such events. These narrations weren't really in confidence since everyone in the community knew about them at the time. It's only today that anybody might object.

11 Jan 1871

"Today we were in meeting, but our church is in a sad situation. Our deacon, John L. Gehman [1819-1892] revealed himself to me several weeks ago as an adulterer, which had already taken place several years ago, with the maid who was with Ihst. She told Ihst about it, but Ihst did not wish to say anything; yet he talked about it so much so that it made me wonder; then he told me about it himself.

Oh dear brother and fellow laborer in the Lord's vineyard, you wouldn't believe how much trouble this caused for me, and also for many others, especially the family. His wife thinks she can bear it with the help of God, yet for the rest of her life can have no more joy."

John L. Gehman had been ordained a deacon at Hereford in 1858. His father was the preacher John Z. Gehman who became inactive after 1848, superseded by John B. Bechtel. Gehman had grown up in the community, was about 50 when this fancy took him! To make matters worse, he had married two sisters from the same family, Susanna Stauffer in 1844 and Elizabeth in 1847. He had one child with the first wife, a daughter, and three sons with the second. It was such a small world that this daughter had married the same Ehst (John M., 1844-1923) with whose maid Gehman conducted the affair. No wonder the family is distressed. Two of John L. Gehman's sons also were deacons. At least his sin was a known one, but worse was in the offing.

11 Jan 1876

"Dear brother and sister, I think the saddest part you have likely heard, of which I would rather not write because it is nothing good, but since it has happened I will mention a little about it, that brother John Gabel fell into an abominable sin and is discharged from the church. This took place while he was still in the state of widowhood.

"...Don't forget us in your prayers. Pray for me and the church. We all need your prayers. Also pray for J. Gabel. He is in great sorrow yet there are those who press him farther down. Old father Gabel was here today and he wept over his son. Today is the 14th."

The sin is "abominable" so could be just anything, the idea being that it is better left unnamed. But far worse, while John L.

Gabel (1837 – 1887) may be a "brother," he is also the son-in-law of
Andrew Mack, having married Mack's daughter Elizabeth.
Gabel's first wife, Leah High, died 23 Aug 1873 at age 34. Andrew
Mack officiated at the funeral. Eight children were born of that first
marriage, 4 of the second.

Gabel had only just been ordained a deacon at Hereford 17 Oct 1872
(Wenger, 262). Gabel's father, Abraham was then old but still living.
He lived till age 86 in 1885, two years before his son died in a
sawmill accident. In 1871 Abraham and J.L. Gabel bought the
Gleason company machinery and begun production of spokes and
tool handles.

This letter came two and a half years after the death of
Gabel's first wife. That his transgression occurred while he was still
a widower, indicates that he was remarried to Andrew Mack's
daughter at the time of this report. The pain of two deacons going
awry in the same small congregation must have been a trial for the
bishop to be. We can imagine that these were not the only such
occurrences. That Gabel was discharged from the church indicates
that there was a discipline intact. Among the charges and counter
charges popular among 19th century Mennonites vs. Reformed
Mennonites, the list of concerned offenses is often limited to slander,
dissension, drunkenness, crudeness and carousing.

Persecute Yourself

The *Bloody Theatre* has its own explanation for these lapses,
that they are social-political, not psychological, that is, that human
nature is weak. After all, in chorus we can all recite the
psychological excuse, "that which I would not that I do." The cause
of their falling away was that they were not being persecuted
enough, had let down their guard and been seduced by the world:

"as soon as a little breathing time set in, they again began to lean towards the world; the parents became rich, the children luxurious and wanton; the world caressed them, and in course of time they became respected and lifted up; the reproach of the cross was relinquished, and the honor of this world stepped into its place." (362).

If this solution to seduction seems medieval, that is the ultimate irony of having for your source of inspiration a book of tortures. There was also a lot of Catholic mysticism mixed in. *Martyr's Mirror* which says "if you then find that the time of freedom has given liberty and room to your lusts, persecute yourself, crucify and put yourself to death, and offer up soul and body to God." (361).

In this law of the excluded middle the Mennonite understanding was that "true Christians have never persecuted the innocent, but were always persecuted themselves" (357). In the absence of persecution, to be saved from the world contagion, the "defenseless" Mennonite must become his own persecutor:

"though outward persecutions now and then cease, yet every Christian is called to sufferings and conflicts...each must live, not after the flesh, but after the Spirit; each must suffer in the flesh, that he may cease from sin." (361).

This suffering of the flesh led to the modern Mennonite predicament in America, asked and re-asked with its corollary, can I give up my life and how profoundly can I persecute myself? Such questions produce weekly calls to repentance and self doubt. The default conclusion was that there was no better way to persecute yourself than to accuse yourself of being unworthy, guilty, weak, that you don't measure up. It can be a theology for oppressing others as well, for if you don't measure up, how could they?

Catechisms of the Survivor

Catechisms of the survivor require that we "examine...whether...you have not lent your tongue to please frivolous, worldly men with vain and useless talk...whether you did not defame your neighbor's good name...by lying and deceit ministered to avarice" (361-62). Both freedom and religion are full of contradiction. Anabaptist martyrs of all kinds played a positive role in the background of the freedoms of civilization. These freedoms depended on lives being sacrificed to break the monolithic Church and Empire. But what is the answer for the descendants of these martyrs if the very freedoms that stem from their sacrifice become the corruptions that defeat them?

Gelassenheit

The way out of this predicament for Mennonites was *gelassenheit*, that is, self surrender. *Gelassenheit* for the martyr, *gelassenheit* for the farmer. The idea is simple enough, not unique to Mennonites, not even confined to one word, (*leidenderweis, seelenfrieden*), but it thoroughly contradicts the modern idea of self realization. *Gelassenheit* is associated with the mystical death of the contemplative life. Whether the product of this mystical union or the result, several roads lead to the its destination.

Certainly the writings of the *Martyr's Mirror* and other contemporary Anabaptists are abstracted into examples of it, but the New Testament is its primary source, although the word does not appear there. From the instance of Christ's humbling himself to the form of a servant, to Paul's "crucifixion with Christ" *gelassenheit* is a sacrifice of self-will, a loss of self exaltation. And it is an active state, so when Ridley, the Oxford martyr, puts out his hand into the fire in 1555, not waiting for it to consume him, that is *gelassenheit*. "Michael Sattler's well known letter in *Martyr's Mirror* to the brotherhood at Horb, sent out of his prison in May 1527 says, 'In this peril I completely surrendered myself unto the will of the Lord, and ... prepared myself even for death for His testimony.'"(cited in the *Mennonite Encyclopedia*) Likewise Hans van Overdam wrote from his prison to the authorities of Gent in 1550:

> "We would rather through the grace of God suffer our temporal bodies to be burned, drowned, racked, or tortured, as it may seem good to you, or be scourged, banished, or driven away, or robbed of our goods, than to show any obedience contrary to the word of God, and we will be patient therein, committing vengeance to God, for we know that He says vengeance belongeth to me, I will recompense" (*Mennonite Encyclopedia*).

But outside of martyrdom a very large part of *gelassenheit* signified brotherly love in communal setting, thus also sharing, which affected Mennonites in every way, even in the choosing of their leaders by lot.

When it signifies surrender to God's will, the language is misunderstood if it is assumed that everything that is is God's will. So it is not God's will per se that is submitted to, rather it is God to whom the soul surrenders. When the un-*gelassenheit* question asks why some things occur, why do bad things happen to good people, *gelassenheit* means surrendering that question.

There are some synthetic *gelassenheits* available in case the real one is too rigorous. It has been taken as a kind of zen state, a personal attitude without reference to persecution or community, "you wait for the answer to show itself… you wait for ideas and experience to come to fruition… you prepare yourself for the unexpected. (Eric Brende, Radical Congruency.com.), But the Mennonite idea had nothing to do with zen or the idea of *Gelassenheit* by Martin Heidegger (1959), it being totally derived from the rigor of such biblical sources as Abraham's sacrifice of Isaac.

The *Mennonite Encyclopedia* says that "present-day Mennonitism has lost the idea of *Gelassenheit* nearly completely," but Mennonites are still preoccupied with the idea of whether and how they can give up their lives.

Bonhoeffer

Mennonites do not face this quandary alone. Psychiatrist Robert Coles agonized over Dietrich Bonhoeffer's resistance to the Nazis and his execution just before the war's end the same way modern Mennonites have over their martyrs. When asked "what would you do under such circumstances, under Hitler, if you were there, back then," Robert Coles could only reply, "by the time that question had been put to the class, not one of us was able to answer with any moral confidence" (Coles, 198-99). That is exactly the Mennonite dilemma.

Cole cites his teacher Reinhold Niebuhr to the effect that there is a "potential disparity" between psychiatry and religion. But it is impossible to counsel "social adjustment" to Mennonites or individuals like Bonhoeffer who are diametrically opposed to accommodation. The disparity of psychiatry and religion is not "potential," it is actual. Counseling stresses adjustment to "normality." Accommodate and you get promotion, but only if you do not continue "the essential 'madness'… that won't settle for the rewards of social conformity." Bonhoeffer's friends at Union Seminary couldn't counsel him out of it, so he returned to Germany, opposed Hitler and was killed. In similar fashion the martyred Mennonites were social heroes.

Niebuhr says. "we looked up to him as if he'd been sent to inspire us (Cole, 201)," but they didn't go back to Germany with him. As Crito does Socrates, they urge Bonhoeffer to escape. Neither did the Mennonite martyrs give in. Why not? They could have lived.

There is something more than life, says Socrates, *the difficulty my friends, is not to avoid death, but to avoid unrighteousness; for that runs faster than death.*

But Niebuhr, Cole, Crito, like the modern Mennonite congregations of the new world, the audience far and wide, see the problem as outside them, focused by someone else, not within themselves as their own problem.

The Dilemma

This externalized conscience creates a dilemma. Either you suffer or you're of the devil they tell you in Mennonite Sunday School. Mennonites in the class mourn their own weakness, claim they can't chose. Moments of rhetorical weakness occur everywhere. In describing this account a woman confided she had wanted to be a missionary as a girl until Jim Eliot and his friends were killed by the Auca Indians. Then she asked herself whether she was willing to die to be a missionary. The answer being no she gave it up and has considered herself a coward ever since, through breast cancer, divorce, child rearing. The test isn't really whether or not you could die, but whether you can live.

What would you do? Die or betray! There is endless guilt and thousands of words. Ethical offenders moralize the purpose of life within. How does it get within? They don't teach that one. But the social hero is commonplace among the population in small ways, in unnoticed acts of surrender. The conscience is not outside but in life's actions. What makes an intellectual anyway but doubt? If it comes to debate, the response to such observations is *ad hominium*, what have you ever done, one will say, as if heroism were a public relations ploy, as if you cannot see in the face of a man his acts.

This whole controversy between inner and the outer smacks of those now discredited Anabaptist pietists, including Mennonites, who were also wholly inner in their motives. They did not fit in the social adjustment franchise, but their attitudes and actions were a major part of Mennonite and Pennsylvania Dutch thinking to 1850. Their influence is said to end about 1850, after at least two hundred years, because that date is selected as their assassination by the anti-pietist Albrecht Ritschl in his *History of Pietism*, which "has been so overpowering and far-reaching that today, outside the small circle of specialists, pietism is still generally associated with anti-intellectualism, hyper-individualism, and holy-group separatists. (Oberman, xii). This "antagonism was continued by the Protestant dialectical theologians of this century, chief among whom was Karl Barth" (Peter Erb in *Arndt*, 1).

It would be a good joke to call Socrates anti-intellectual and Bonhoeffer too. Pietists were anti-intellectual because they wouldn't be persuaded, hyper-individual because they insisted on their own way, holy-group separatists because they thought they were as right as their opponents. In the end anyone can be a martyr. Just give it all up, *gelassenheit*. Surrender. Which is not to say that tests of the self-seeking masses don't occur in their racist thoughts, in the crucifixions of their depressing assessments of their lives without faith, the sacrifice of their children's lives for one Moloch or another. Who wants to be a moral hero? Everyone. Who doubts their commitment to that end? Everyone.

Socrates

There is a lot of talk about the death of philosophers in the *Phaedo*, whether and what kind of death they should seek. The logic can be applied to the martyrs. It all amounts to a conflict between the soul and the body. When the body reigns then the soul is in recession but when the soul rules the body is kept under. Hence Socrates says that it is a contradiction that a philosopher should fear death, for then he would be closest to his highest aspirations. This also sums the Mennonite problem.

The psychologists of that world the Mennonites disdain have raised another inquiry over their failure to accommodate, whether or not Mennonites were not just harboring a death wish by making people murder them, let alone that they should be so filled with self-loathing that they should persecute themselves.

This death wish charge could occur with every principled stand. If only the stubborn would let go of that fixed idea we could let them live in peace. That we might let them live at all is of course the catch, for by what right do we rule? Conformity. Accommodation. On very similar grounds I. F. Stone charges that Socrates committed suicide in a deliberate aggravation of those judges in the jury of 500. Stone equivocates the state's execution of sentence upon the defendant into his own suicide, a peppery modern insight in an age where no power equals rationalization.

Socrates can answer also for the Mennonites. He says, *me you have killed because you wanted to escape the accuser and not to give an account of your lives* (Jowett). That is the point of course. We will all start to sound like Mennonites if the world can do anything to anybody in order to avoid facing itself and then blame you for it. Is the It-Self here a difficult idea?

The It-Self is every institution of government, science and religion that puts the individual to death for not conforming. In Mennonite terms the unclean garments the It-Self dresses in are just opposite the garments of the Lamb the Mennonites claim to wear.

Socrates says he wants to do nothing common or mean when in danger, nor to use any cowardly way of escaping death, even in war, so he refuses escape and all the petty escapes of his sentence urged upon him. Had he lived later in Switzerland he could have been drowned in a bag.

How do Mennonites answer the charge that they are persecuting themselves because they are filled with self-loathing? Well they could deny self-loathing as a misstatement of their position. But take another look. The Mennonite point is that the inner world is forced to integrity when the outer is threatened. And vice versa, that when all is tranquil the certainty of the inner world evaporates, overcome by the every day.

Prison Camp

Prison literatures tend to take these views. The best fiction, like Solzhenitsyn's, is dense with detail, absorbed totally in the present sensation. But in reality imprisonment is just opposite this, there is no action, no work detail, no comrades, there is loneliness, suffering, vacancy and an infinite time to doubt. That is why Ivan Denisovich keeps moving, it keeps him sane. But his life is packed into one day, the real prisoners' lives are packed into an age and it is an age of suffering.

The point about the martyrs is that they do not know their end, but the outer fire of persecution wonderfully focuses their thoughts. Consider Viktor Frankl's three years in the death camps. Each small choice saves his life. Each expression of intent heals. The inane falls away. Each breath is a new existence. Compare that with the life of one with every expectation of the commonplace continuing. A meal, a bed, a bath, ordinary greetings. This is one you can corrupt. So the Martyr Book is sharpening to the edge that each commonplace must be miraculous, each moment a gratitude.

Early American Mennonites

If these very psychological questions still seem to preoccupy Mennonites, their forebearers were not so different. In the old world they took Mennonites to death and to prison. The new world was a more happy occasion, but still with consequences, because the lawless think: "you can steal their cow and they won't prevent it! What do you say about going over and getting some corn?"

It was thought you could do just anything to Mennonites. In early Pennsylvania there were roving bands of the lawless doing just that. They burned out Conrad Weiser, who was no Mennonite. His father-in-law Muhlenberg says "if the head of a house should give offense to some insolent Irishman or brutal German, he may very likely find that some harm has been done to his cattle or crops during the night" (I, 136). Of the French and Indian War Wenger says "there is no evidence that Mennonites used self-defense in any attack made upon them" (58).

For the evil-doer the only danger at all in bothering Mennonites was in calculating who among them were truly devout, thus defenseless and nonresistant. The cry of the devout, "vengeance is mine, I will repay" echoed with "because he loves me, says the Lord, I will rescue him." But human contradiction can be as great a force as piety so there was always a danger that the thief might come upon a lapsed Mennonite or a husband Marvin and get a beating.

Mennonites seriously rejected the worldly constants of self defense and revenge. They would not swear an oath and would not go against the oaths of previous generations who had sworn oaths, even if that were wrong. They declined the oath of loyalty to renounce the British government in 1777, not because they loved the British, or because, contradictorily, Jesus said, "swear not at all," but they feared being "forsworn."

Such incredible literalists held their fathers' or grandfathers' promises to King George as binding upon themselves. But they were always hostage to the times and fears of torture that their bloody book fostered. Friends and neighbors in Pennsylvania came to their defense, said "their present blindness to their own essential interest proceeds from an unhappy bias in their education, [taking Jesus and martyrdom literally] and not from a disaffection to the present Government" (Wenger, 61). On the whole the Americans were willing to blink an eye.

If the government blinked the Mennonite bishops did not. Though they were against swearing and war, the Franconia Conference favored loyalty to the British Crown because of their previous promise (oath) of loyalty. When Mennonite Bishop Christian Funk favored the Pennsylvania constitution because it gave freedom of worship and promised to exempt from arms and the oath and also favored paying a war tax to the American government which the other ministers opposed, he was deposed (1778). Too insistent upon the truth. He is still blamed for intransigence and pride.

Questioning Righteousness

So roses have thorns and Mennonites mud, which is to say that the survivals into the 20th century by small farm communities of these introversions and even further are nearly miraculous, even to get along as well as they did. They had no recourse to present day amnesias like movies and air conditioning. Why then do moderns fail in their burdens of righteousness, fall to porn? The strait gates again.

If we apply doubt, question their righteousness with an anti-Petrarchan view of it as later Elizabethans did of beauty, it is not to magnify their contradictions but to "show the adverse party as the advocate," as Shakespeare's Sonnet XXXV urges. So Mennonites were as deeply conflicted as any principled people were, "clouds and eclipses stain both moon and sun / And loathsome canker lives in sweetest bud." The ideal cloys. It is boring until we turn it on its head to see what really is true. Maybe good humor is more tolerant than law. Maybe it is the only true love, to see realistically the clay feet about which not much is said, not to hide the ills, indeed those were confessed openly, but to urge "no more be grieved at that which thou hast done." But Mennonites didn't say this much or anything much; it wasn't in their nature.

Social vs. Personal

Mennonites occupy the opposite end of the spectrum from Evangelicals who talk religion a lot. Mennonite historian John Ruth says that Evangelicals proclaimed their experience of personal conversion, but left speed, progress, and democracy unexamined. Mennonites "missed, in much talk of it, a carrying through of certain practical conclusions" (239).

Isaac Horst says the Old Mennonites thought the modern evangelistic movements "tolerated and encouraged pride and inflated self-esteem" (29). Notwithstanding their many contradictions, the Mennonites' "practical conclusions" defaulted them into the unlikely status of heroes of the social conscience, asking questions and taking actions while the rest of society was idle and self bound.

For Ruth another tension between Mennonites and Evangelicals was because, after 1850, Mennonites were forever turning into them. The social, not the personal was the Mennonite reason for being. "Christianity consists as much in accepting and maintaining 'a right fellowship,' as in sensing an inner drama," says Ruth (239). Mennonites viewed their "right fellowship" as a kind of millennial reign, chiliasm again. They thought the church must make "cosmic reconciliation visible in terms of a human order."

If this didn't sound so fine it would seem hyperbolic. Such ideas can also be blamed on the New Testament. The Mennonite Church was a "colony of heaven" opposing national, technological, and cultural patterns (239), which does away with patriotism, voting and public office, and unless you were a straggler, stocks and bonds, yes? These were stranger and pilgrim Christians, alienated from the world to God. If the social order of the Mennonites is called "a right fellowship" it almost sounds like it could be a round fellowship of knights.

Absolute Soul Liberty

Just when we think the Mennonites are wanting they slip through the net. "Absolute soul liberty," was the first of all their values. With this immensely appealing phrase Wenger adds that their great error was that "they were just three centuries ahead of their time." He says that as refugees in England between 1550-1600 they brought "Anabaptist ideas such as religious freedom, separation of church and state, nonresistance and non swearing of oaths" (6). Mennonites aren't much credited for being "at least partially responsible for the rise of the Friends and Baptist churches, for these groups adopted these [Anabaptist] doctrines as a whole or in part" (6).

Mennonites taught English Baptists adult baptism and universal atonement. Their persecutors, the Reformed, believed in a "limited" atonement. They taught Baptists the nonhierarchical liberty of conscience and the principle of religious freedom. They communicated with the Quakers' inner light, took no oaths, were nonresistant to aggression. They demonstrated to the Congregationalists local autonomy and to everybody the idea that theological statements are not as significant as human conduct. Bold and appealing stuff.

Quakers

When nineteenth century America was preoccupied with human rights abuses, Mennonites of the 17th century, five years after their arrival in 1683, took on the Quakers with this world class declaration:"…ye Quackers doe here handel men, licke they handel there ye Cattel…we contradict & are against this traffick of menbody." This heroic Mennonite doctrine of 1688 was way ahead of its time: "there is a saying, that we shall doe to all men, like as we will be done our selves; making no difference of what generation, descent or Color they are. And those who steal or rob men, and those who buy or purchase them, are they not all a like?" ("The Germantown Antislavery Protest", Wenger, 413).

Visionaries

When you examine the circumstances it sounds very much like these people were the most extraordinary social visionaries. In a trust agreement of 1725, Mennonites began their new world social welfare. One hundred acres of donated land in Skippack were set aside for all citizens to provide a school, burial ground, meetinghouse and for the benefit of the poor. This was the school where Christopher Dock taught. Mennonites, first among all Protestants, loved nature, grew crops, opposed war and helped alien, oppressed peoples. We almost want to say they were the first ecologists.

These aren't peasant attitudes, in case somewhere there is a Mennonite who wonders where he or she got their mind. The Mennonite mind sprang from taking the gospel really literally, producing their concern for others' well being, their sense of justice and mercy. But it also arose from their faith and the fire of persecution. As said, suffering creates soul.

Pennsylvania religion differed from New England. The hillbilly fervor of liberty really appealed to them. They were conflicted by principle, full of contradiction, lawlessly insisting on their law. Mennonites were in many ways the most morally attractive of these religious sects. They applied the highest and best prophetic principles, *Is it not to share your food with the hungry, and to provide the poor wanderer with shelter—when you see the naked to clothe him, and not to turn away from your own flesh and blood?* They applied God to the foolish and ungrateful, the widow, orphan, alien. Even if they levied more astringent principles on themselves, it was a group think to delight any utopian founder. *Is not this the kind of fasting I have chosen? To loose the chains of injustice and untie the cords of the yoke, to set the oppressed free and break every yoke?*

No Credit

So Mennonites gave their lives and took away an extreme self-loathing to their own pride, evidence that their ideas were greater than their own glory. *Gelassenheit.* That they could ever speak ill of their past confirms in the present both a lack of education and extreme anti-worldly bias. The stereotype holds that "no credit was taken for a good deed done; no record made of achievements indicating the possession of ability above the ordinary. If a church was built, no record of those subscribing, no mention of the committee through whose efforts the funds were obtained or under whose supervision the work was done were preserved. If a book was printed the author's name was not disclosed." (*History of the Longacre-Longaker-Longenecker Family*, 22).

This was the view as of 1900. By 2000 there seemed to be a lot of records, even if peculiar, names carved into attic beams, as in the case of Abraham L. Reiff of Worcester, or written in an Alms Book. And maybe their letters, like in the Jacob Mensch collection, were inaccessible, but still in typically introverted Mennonite style they had been translated. You just had to ask for them nicely, something Mennonites have had a hard time doing.

If we say that human beauty and righteousness have a defect, then Mennonites, with a huge credit balance in social action, oppressed themselves in order to maintain their fellowship, produced significant disagreements over coats and bonnets, suspicions of technology, were as hard on themselves as they were a blessing to the world around them. There was no anonymity in their austerity and self control, they were expected to conform to fellowship. Conflicted by the same self doubt that so damages self expression in art, "I celebrate myself, I sing myself," was just the opposite of their aim. The temptation to rebel, to explore the ocean of creativity unleashed by the new freedoms of Pennsylvania, caused them to join in the greater context the Pennsylvania Dutch, for no matter what the case, *exuberance is still beauty*.

Public service ads against marijuana, alcohol and tobacco, turn out to be entirely Mennonite in spirit. We foresee these same ads in a millennial future decreeing:

"Just say no to anger, no to pride!"

"Why wait, say no to stupidity now."

Mennonites were the underground resistance against the corruption of the world, called themselves the nonresistant, meaning they resisted war, but their resistance was strong against the world, if somewhat boring. In mockery of the world they didn't vote, hold office, sue, write, paint or read. Their children, even grandmothers maybe, wanted some fun by 1900. That feeling has come full circle today; some Mennonite organizations think they need to expunge the name Mennonite because it does not appeal to any known demographic, it's just confused with the Amish. Mennonites never got much following among the rich and famous. They still don't; they have attracted the disenfranchised peacenik. Mennonites were in the right country for utopian experiments. But surely nobody ever wanted to be a Mennonite just to submit their will to Conference.

Two Targets

So they have had two targets on their chests, submit to conference or else, lay down your life and persecute yourself. Illogical as it sounds, with two centuries of horrors behind them in the old world, ten American generations can wonder in varying degree whether they would have had the courage now to have sacrificed themselves then, so they are held hostage by the European martyrs, denied the peaceful fruits of the very freedom their ancestors died to secure. "Could you forfeit your life as they did" was and is asked in Sunday schools and small groups, at church dinners. Who can say? When you start giving your life over to what not to conform to, where do you stop anyway? Die to wear a beard? To be sprinkled, immersed? To publicly confront authority. To speak a certain language? Where does inalienable freedom not force us to go in its quest?

Leaders of a group sacrifice themselves in varying degrees. Don't they feel that the greatest sacrifice must also obtain for the least? That means you could go to death as much from the tyranny of your own group who made you conform, as from the oppressor. Who were the most effective resistance for the Gaza Strip settlers when Israel evicted them? Teenagers, girls at that. Can the group not confront the dominant group without your death? After the fact of copious European tortures the question for American Mennonites was whether they too would, over issues of how to worship God, leave their flesh upon the posts.

A great number of Mennonite immigrants to Montgomery County Pennsylvania were Swiss, not Dutch and not *Deitsch*, meaning German, but still they are called Pennsylvania Dutch. They were Pietists or anti-pietists, Schwenkfelders or Sabbatarians, Dunkers, Brethren, Quakers, Lutherans, Moravians, rebaptizers or Reformed and if they weren't that maybe they were Mennonites. Pennsylvania attracted that cream of diversity disaffected American liberals once went to Canada.

The Dream

What could be more a part of the American Mennonite dream than to found an ideal agrarian society in advance of Hawthorne's *Blithedale Romance* and *Walden* I and II and Commune III, except this one was part democracy, part theocracy? It had government, order, rules, enforcement. Mennonites are like Jews when they're not acting like Mormons.

Works Cited

The Bloody Theater or Martyrs Mirror of the Defenseless Christians. Thieleman J. van Braght, tr. from the Dutch ed. Of 1660 by Joseph F. Sohm. Scottdale, Pa.: Mennonite Publishing House, 1964.

Robert Coles. *Lives of Moral Leadership*. NY: Random House, 2000.

Don Dedera. *Navajo Rugs*. Flagstaff: Northland Press. 1975

Peter Erb in Johann Arndt, *True Christianity*. NY: Paulist Press, 1979.

Viktor E. Frankl, *Man's Search for Meaning*. Boston: Beacon Press. 1966

History of the Longacre-Longaker-Longenecker Family, 1902.

Isaac R. Horst. *A Separate People*. Waterloo: Herald Press, 2000.

The Letters of Andrew Mack, excerpted from the Jacob B. Mensch Letter Collection in the Mennonite Heritage Center, translated by Isaac R. Horst.

The Mennonite Encyclopedia (Friedmann, Robert. "Gelassenheit." Canadian Mennonite Encyclopedia Online. 1955. Mennonite Historical Society of Canada.)

Heiko A. Oberman. *Johann Arndt, True Christianity*, NY: Paulist Press, 1979.

John L. Ruth. *Maintaining the Right Fellowship*. Scottdale: Herald Press, 1984.

I.F. Stone. *The Trial of Socrates*. Boston: Little, Brown & Co. 1988.

J. C. Wenger. *History of the Mennonites of the Franconia Conference*. Scottdale, Pa.: Mennonite Publishing House, 1985.

The Image of God

Education in the Inner World

It is partly a myth that Mennonite ministers were uneducated. They had no more education as ministers than they had as teachers, but started many first churches and schools in Pennsylvania. Their "preachers" were chosen by lot, never knew in advance who they were going to be. This selection process was an advantage because it provided an instant infrastructure of frontier folk churches, pastors, cemeteries and schools while the hierarchical Lutheran and the Reformed had to wait to be supplied from abroad.

Some Mennonite ministers were boring, had no gift at all for teaching or speaking, let alone scholarship. John Z. Gehman (1793-1882) felt he was not the right man for the job so he read from the sermons of Denner (Wenger, 263). Sometimes Mennonites struck gold, measured by the names in the roster of the Alms Book or the quality of publications they issued. Especially where they had flourished a long time, like Skippack and Hereford, a hundred years by 1830, there was family mentoring.

Members of extended family who came into this enviable style of ministry kept a supply of the best and brightest work that had inspired Mennonites from the beginning. Such families were often interrelated, for example Elizabeth Bechtel (1852-1885) married Henry Mack, brother of Andrew Mack, while her father, John B. Bechtel, ordained Andrew Mack to the ministry. There being only a slight separation of pastor and flock, discussion of the main topics of religion was commonplace, even if in German. It was more or less the preoccupation of every Mennonite family.

This lack of education was reversed when it came to the inner world. Mennonites imbibed precise judgments of right behavior, and judging from their visionary status in providing social relief for orphans, schools, prophetic stands against slavery and their dedication to an inoffensive and defenseless lifestyle, Mennonites might claim to be as educated inwardly as they were charged with failing outwardly.

Elisabeth Bechtel's Library

A small library of German books found in Anna Elizabeth's Media attic in 2004 includes some texts of Mennonite education. The books had belonged to the whole family of Bechtels 175 years before, maternal forbearers of our folk genius.

Writings favored by Mennonites for two centuries especially included John Arndt's *Wahren Christenthem* of 1605 and Jan Philip Schabaelje's *Die Wandelnde Seele* of 1634. These argued for a more personal piety, immersion in the spring of living water, as they might put it. Arndt especially was the major secular text of Mennonite inner life. In the attic editions Arndt and Schabaelje occurred in printings of 1832 and 1833 respectively. Finding them made necessary an effort to understand 17th century Mennonite and pietistic thinking.

The books have several ownership inscriptions, Elisabeth Bechtel's, her mother, father, grandfather and some neighbors. One has her husband's name stamped in it, two have been inscribed by her daughter, Anna Mack. Among German/English and German new testaments, Mennonite song books and catechisms of the 1870's, the earlier works of the 1830's and one of 1745 are the most important.

There being multiple generations of pastors in the Bechtel family, other volumes would have also been in their possession.

These, kept by Elisabeth Bechtel, could be explained by early mortalities in the family, except that she also died prematurely in 1885 at age 33. The books are almost the sole personal remains of three generations, Abraham Bechtel, John B. Bechtel, and Elisabeth Bechtel.

How did the older books come to Elisabeth's possession after her death? John B. Bechtel (1807-1889) and Mary Longacre Bechtel (1814-1898) had eight children. Five died before their parents, including Elisabeth. The best answer is that Mary Bechtel, Elisabeth's mother, who lived until 1898, left them as a keepsake to her grand daughter, Anna Mack (1880-1970) when she turned 21.

Anna preserved them all her long life and left them in turn to the care of her daughter, Anna Elizabeth Reiff Young (1910-2005). By the grace of these women the books slept and slept again, incognito a hundred years. When asked about their provenance the second Elizabeth said that when she and her mother moved to Media, PA in 1944 her mother took care of the domestic arrangements. She did not know exactly how grandfather Henry Mack's chest got to that attic either, but probably came when he lived with them at the end of his life. The books retained their provenance in themselves. It is not likely they were much opened in that hundred years, but the secrets they hid of their past owners' lives were not lost.

The most important link in the gathering of this library was John B. Bechtel. He acquired Johann Arndt's, *Wahren Christenthem* at the estate sale of his father's library in 1861 and wrote on the endpaper in both English and German, "Bought at the Sale of my dec'd Father Abm. C. Bechtel Nov the 15th 1861 / John B. Bechtel /paid $1.00 / one of the administrators."

His father, Abraham C. Bechtel (1776-1861), born the year of the Declaration of Independence, acquired the book in 1833 and had written on the front pastedown, "Subscriber /Abraham C. Bechtel / January the 26th 1833.

In the extended Bechtel family this Abraham is not to be confused with his own father, the minister Abraham Bechtel (1749-1815) who was trustee in 1780 for an acre of land given by Henry Stauffer for the Colebrookdale meetinghouse, a branch of the Hereford congregation (Wenger, 251, 121).

Four succeeding generations of Bechtels were Mennonite ministers, Abraham Bechtel, Abraham C's brother, Bishop John C. (Clemens) Bechtel (1779-1843), John B. Bechtel (1807-1889), and John B. Bechtel's grandson, Henry G. Bechtel (b. 1878), ordained a minister at Vincent in 1914.

17th Century Mennonite and Pietistic Thinking

Arndt's *Wahren Christenthem* is a very large book. It involves understanding the thoughts and intents of the heart, an inner life Mennonites didn't talk about but practiced. Scholars call such preoccupations, the mystical life. It was the basis of Mennonite participation in the spiritual worlds. As they might say, Mennonites wanted to share in *the fellowship of his suffering and be conformed to the image of His death*, their motive from the beginning.

What can the subscription and possession of John Arndt's *Wahren Christenthem* tell us about Abraham Bechtel? We long for more than bare facts to represent these early lives. The inscriptions and signatures and books give a place to start, but the contents are really the only means of reconstruction available.

The physical copy retrieved from the attic library has two parts bound in one, 941 and 232 pages respectively, and two copper-engraved title pages with 63 full-page woodcut emblems. Three German editions appeared in Philadelphia and Germantown prior to this one of 1832: Ben Franklin's (1751), Christopher Saur's (1765) and one printed by Johann Georg Ritter, 1830.

The inferences are speculative. What made *Wahren Christenthem* the most frequently used devotional book for more than two centuries among Mennonites? There was a conscious use of it in daily and devotional life. In mid 18th century Pennsylvania, Muhlenberg wrote of Arndt in the same breath as the Bible: "she continued to study her Bible and Arndt's True Christianity" (I, 219) "…take hold of the Holy Bible and True Christianity every day."

The Inner Life

The central principle of Arndt's book is that the inner life, the thought life, is maintained by continuous meditation of the good. Many prerequisites for a conscious inner life exist, yet at the same time there are no prerequisites. Minds are constantly dreaming alternative scenarios, planning, visualizing their activities, except that these activities are often only fears, fantasies and vanities. That is, they are wholly negative. How to turn the thought life positive is a major concern of Arndt.

No Work

A study of the different ways schools direct their seekers toward a proper inner world enlightenment shows one principle above all else, the work itself, that there is work and it is work. Zazen. Pray. Rituals. Records. Exotic and esoteric exercises. Imbibe the lotus. Work.

Arndt's signpost on the road to light is, stop, don't work. The schools say you should feel guilty if you don't work. Absence of effort was perceived as anti-intellectualism in the 19th century and got Arndt into trouble among rationalist critics. Many who take the way of work and self improvement are indeed the best and brightest.

They form the elite just because of their hard work. Likewise because of their hard work they cannot credit not working toward enlightenment. But to him *that does not work....*

A local talk show host once offered the opposite of these words to a poet who had volunteered to open the mysteries of Herbert, Hopkins and Donne on the air. The host was ready to book the engagement by phone, but the poet suggested meeting first. Increasingly personal questions revealed that this poet was unemployed, which got the talk host a little peppery. He volunteered that if a man will not work, let him not eat. After the poet paid for the lunch he came upon the oddest sentence, *to the man who does not work, but trusts God who justifies the wicked, his faith is credited as righteousness.* This could have been right out of Arndt.

Contrary

But there is a difficult contrary principle to this inner life, that these thoughts maintained by continuous meditation of the good are opposed, undermined, and reversed by the counterfeit words of the very people who do work at the thing. Arndt means that the leaders are the chief obstacles. It's like your teenager railing about hypocrites, except that Arndt was born in 1555. If it is not work, what is it?

The Inexplicable Event

The beginning attribute of the good occurs in what scholars call the "mystical union," but it's almost as though you wake up one day to suddenly possess it. The interior life begins in an inexplicable event, a little like birth, a thing suddenly appearing. That is, union begins in the beginning and is not the end of some process. The notion is counter-intuitive to work. It seems more rational to suppose that union were the result of efforts and exercises, achieved after much seeking, that this is the end, not the beginning of the process.

The irony that union is accomplished through union, not by effort but effortlessness, is like backing a horse into the stable forwards.

What illustrates duality in physics illustrates unity in Arndt, that is, it is a problem of language to speak of doing and not doing simultaneously. By analogy to wave and particle motion, whose expression the physicist Heisenberg calls a problem of language, illustrated by the dual character of matter and radiation, "it is obvious that a thing cannot be a form of wave motion and composed of particles at the same time-the concepts are too different" (10-11). Since Arndt places mystical union at the beginning of life, not the end, the three steps frequently offered in analysis of mystical union, that is, purgation, illumination, and union need to be reversed. The order should be, union, illumination, purgation.

Union, Illumination, Purgation.

Purgation involves a change of habit, but it is not negative. Purgation is in fact perfection, or better, a progressive perfecting. The aforementioned counterfeits also reverse the order of things, put purgation first, not last. Viewed as an outward change of habit, purgation as change of speech, dress and habits impress upon a group the identity of a desired member. If you don't look, talk and act like a ball player, you must not be one. Substitute corporate lawyer or school teacher to see if this isn't the ritual of membership. Arndt turns this on its head, mystically speaking, so that anybody with purgation already in hand, who walks, talks and acts properly is not at the beginning but at the end of the three steps, a senior member, not a beginner. The joke of the counterfeit is that the true ones are outwardly the same as the counterfeits who are not one at all. Go figure.

Illumination

It is offensive to common sense to have illumination in a rough state of being. Arndt's point is that you can't have it any other way. Union occurs to the grossly undeserving. Illumination occurs in that nasty state. Only *after* union and illumination begin to be assimilated can reformation, purgation, perfection begin. This assimilation takes time. Union may occur in a second and perfection in a century.

This reversal made Arndt loved by the Pennsylvania Dutch and the Mennonites, but hated by the rationalists. Any farm hand can get life and illumination? It goes against the grain. There is no social status in identity with farm hands or subscribing to the patently irrational. These pietists were charged with being anti-intellectual, hyper-individual and separatist. But Arndt's appeal celebrates, as do all the Pennsylvania Dutch, the simple glory, praise and magnificence of Christ. Arndt says that "you must be established in Christ through faith and be righteous in him before you can do any good work" (46), that "through the new birth the image of God begins to be slowly renewed...."

The Image of God

A renewal of the image of God is the purpose of the three steps. Union was obtained with no work at all, the work comes in the renewing. Arndt says that "God does not need our service in the slightest way, but our neighbor does" (130).

For Mennonites specifically the renewed image of God involved attitudes that range from *gelassenheit* to humility, the difference being that in the earlier half of their history, *gelassenheit* and martyrhood were either occurring or remembered strongly. By the 19th century, prosperity had replaced martyrdom. Suffering decreased and *gelassenheit* was lower cased to humility, the view taken in the *Mennonite Encyclopedia* where humility means conformity to a plainness of dress. But there is always enough suffering.

Arndt's image of God has nothing to do with plain dress and everything to do with inward yieldedness and surrender. Mennonites tended to take the view that surrendering to overwhelming circumstances was the same as surrendering to God. This idea of surrender was also the source of their defenselessness and pacifism, which they called *the will of God*, a sort of resignation. Their hope was that surrendering to the inevitable would somehow change their destiny. Resignation came either with acceptance, or with triumph when negative circumstances were reversed.

Resignation occurred to a remarkable degree in folk families, especially with our example and her mother, for Elizabeth nearly died in her first year. Anna was resigned to accept this. How many children and adults had died prematurely in this family? More than we counted here: five children of the Bechtels, Peter Mack, Anna's brother, Jesse Mack, Kate Rosenberger, two sons of Jacob L., a child of Andrew Mack.

When You Lose Your Puppy

Under modern conditions of reduced sickness and mortality people of the present are more inclined to assert their rights than to surrender. In a disaster they ask, "where was God," as if God were a puppy they had lost. Renewing the image of God begins with an inward attitude of surrender not just to the inevitable, but also in the every day, the writing of a sentence, rescue from harm, telling your family you love them, encouraging people in defeat. Being weak so you can be strong.

Abraham Bechtel's subscription of *Wahren Christenthum* at least tells us that the separation of priesthood and laity was not so great in his time. Any Mennonite might expect to be ordained anytime his name was chosen, which is of course what happened to Abraham's son, John B. Bechtel in 1848. Anyone could serve because it was expected that everyone knew these things, just as anyone could begin this union. How else did these Mennonites claim title to the ineffable peace?

John Bechtel's *Die Wandelnde Seele*

Another important 17th century text among those attic editions is Jan Philip Schabaelje's *Die Wandelnde Seele* (1635). One copy had been heavily inscribed in 1833 by John B. Bechtel, an important name for the provenance of the books, but also for the continuity of the Hereford Mennonites for whom he acted when the lot fell to him during the Oberholtzer schism over church polity. He was ordained to replace Christian Clemmer who went over with the "New" Mennonites. .John B. Bechtel was also later distinguished for his testimony in an Appeal before the Supreme Court of Pennsylvania (Samuel H. Landis Et Al. vs. Henry H. Borneman Et Al.) (1883), unusual for a Mennonite.

The secret life of a mystic is not revealed in the ownership of a book, but he was not a youth when the lot fell on him at age 41. It's not as though he had been yearning for the call either, but his inscriptions in the attic edition suggest he was by then a kind of Mennonite philosopher. His many signatures therein signify more than a statement of simple ownership.

He has signed it three times, first with wife, Mary, on the front pastedown, in English and then in German. Across from these signatures he has written with a flourish, both in English and in German, "Wandering Soul / a very useful book." Then, turning the page, he signs his name large in German in pencil on the verso and on the recto of the second free endpaper, he writes large in ink with a flourish, in English, "John B. Bechtel / February the 13th 1835."

The translated title of the first English translation of 1834 reads, *The Wandering Soul; or, Dialogues Between the wandering Soul and Adam, Noah, and Simon Cleophas Comprising A History of the World, Sacred and Profane From the Creation Until the Destruction of Jerusalem.* Two copies exist in that attic library in German, 1833 and 1834. The 1834 copy has no marks, but that of 1833 is heavily inscribed. A lot like *Wahren Christenthum, Die Wandelnde Seele*, popular among Mennonites, was translated into German and published in seven different editions in Pennsylvania from 1767 to 1833.

It is a more partisan work than *Wahren*, a fictionalized world history told by Cleophas, brother of Joseph. Aspects of *The Wandering Soul* are held today as a counter weight to the chiliast view of the idea of the last days popular with the *Left Behind* series. *The Wandering Soul* has been brought back into print by opponents of the Dispensationalists, that is, the Preterists. They believe the destruction of Jerusalem in 70 AD fulfilled the major part of the Revelation of St. John, that the last days have already been here and gone! *The Wandering Soul*, supports parts of this, especially concerning Jerusalem.

The desire for a deeper more genuine spirituality in these two landmarks of German pietism was appreciated by Mennonites in the 1830s and almost continually among these people who examined every boundary between their faith and the world.

Folk Life Weaving

"All Navajo yarn is spun at least twice; some three and four times (up to ten times for tapestries), with each spinning improving tightness, smoothness and fineness. Foundation yarn called warp, must be respun several times. As the warps are moved back and forth they disappear under the wefts." (Don Dedera. *Navajo Rugs*, 16)

A family and a culture is like a weaving. The foundation yarns, the vertical warps, made firm by extra spinning, are covered by the horizontal wefts. Even the vocabulary of weaving suggests families. The Navajo spindle turns carded wool into "homespun." Families are homespun. Their foundations must be re-spun.

On a Navajo loom the foundation threads are stretched vertically between the upper and lower loom bars before the wefts are horizontally woven. Weaving differs from a family only because when "weaving begins at the bottom," the weaver has a mental image of the complete rug. The family cannot see beyond its present continuation, but it can see everything up to the present, if conditions permit.

The Authority of the Living

Warp strength is analogous to authority in families. Since the family first set the standard the next generation is empowered by the preceding warps to achieve it. The standard seems arbitrary because it is. Family members of different generations combine to form the authority of the living. The ways in which the authorities of the generations are formed is like the re-spinning of Navajo yarn, the foundation of its finished work.

Natural Heir

Anna Elizabeth inherited a mantle of authority from her
mother Anna Mack. The worst you can say of Elizabeth is that in
loving and supporting her mother she was denied many recognitions
that would have come to her, which denials fueled that impeccable
taste and rapier wit.

Anna Elizabeth repaid Anna's privations many times over.
Anna was forced to leave school in the 6th grade at age 12. Anna
Elizabeth Elizabeth, graduated fifth in her high school class at age 15
and immediately went to art school. Anna knew German, Elizabeth
Latin. Anna had a stepmother, Elizabeth had a doting mother. Anna
left home, Elizabeth stayed home. All the good that Anna possessed
she gave to her daughter. The transmission of folk culture was
catalyzed even more greatly when Henry came to live with them
those 8 years until 1944. When they moved from Philadelphia to
Media he went to live with son Philip.

The stories and artifacts, the weavings were preserved
another century because of this. When my mother, Beatrice, was
about to give birth a second time, having one son already, she
expected a daughter, but got a second son, who was then named for
this Anna Elizabeth, and for Andrew Mack, copying her initials. AE.
To me the whole story is a miracle of discovery.

Weaving Begins At The Bottom

Families differ from weavings, cannot see their own end
because the foundation warps are set on the loom before the work
begins. We can't see this and may think we spin the generations spin
one by one. Each generation of a family is required to re-spin itself

into the living tapestry. Future generations must weave from the base already laid. As the generations move up the loom they are woven into what is already there.

"Weaving begins at the bottom" means that the alternating sets of warps disappear under the wefts" (Dedera,18). No good weaver would weave the new *against* the old, but with it. How this happens in families is always of interest, limited only by records and the length of their lives.

Women do the weaving among the Navajo, but women do not weave families alone. Women and men are spun together, mothers and fathers with aunts and uncles new-spin the grandparents' foundation.

With the Pennsylvania Dutch many different families wove by intermarriage the tapestry of folk life from outside and inside the families that extended to a series of communities.

Art For Your Sake

Folk art categories have been defined so we know what to look for in the field and at auction. Books on Pennsylvania Dutch Folk Art and life give a notion of it but it was folk because it was done by ordinary folk, handmade. It was art because their love transformed it. They made it for someone, not for its own sake. They call them Mennonite blanket chests if they have porcelain knobs.

These makers are called "amateurs," but their work was generated from the home not a factory. When you read the sales pitch as to why you should like folk art it sounds like a bunch of nice hobbits: "…chests, spoon racks, children's toys, cradles and small chairs contributed to the picture they have left us of a happy, industrious and religious people who loved their homes and lived in an atmosphere of mutual affection" (Kauffman, 12).

Go to Nebraska, bring old barn wood to Arizona, cobble trestle tables out of cans of old nails. Paint and rub and repaint and re-rub and smooth into a pretty finish as country furniture that imitates folk art, but there is also an authentic. In the trade, barn decorations are worth good bucks, cast iron stove plates, weather vanes, pie plates, tin ware, copper and brass, homespun, linens, show towels, samplers, quilts. It's possible to even sell hand made bricks. But if folk art comes on the market there must be something wrong with it, because the best is kept, either that or somebody's selling a heritage made specifically for them. After all, who is Margaret Gehman (1851)? Oh, I know, she's the lady that made that tulip that blooms from the heart. When people sell treasures previous generations loved, especially those handmade, they end up at flea markets.

But sometimes people are angry at the past and that's why they dispose of it. Other times they are ignorant. I saw a lady sell three original Chagall watercolors for a $150 because she didn't know! When it comes to settling the estates of the departed, either nobody cares or family members compete for valuables. When they get the remains home they put them away and the next generation sells it at a flea market. There is little conservation after the fact, little inventory, measurements, acid free envelopes.

Remember all these lives weaving their destinies together? Folk art proceeds from that. It includes everything. But most of it got used up. Fabric wore out, kitchen pots rusted, pottery broke. To apply the term in a more proper sense, folk art is any aspect of folk life that still exists, a thing folk did themselves, whether decorated or not, to sustain their lives. It was a folk art to butcher a pig, plow a field, build a barn. It's folk art to cook a meal, make a quilt and children's clothes, even if they don't go to market. It's folk art at the forge, folk speech in the field, in the kitchen and in the shed. What are they doing in that shed? Making distal finks? It's folk art when the itinerant comes round to charcoal sketch the children. If made for its own use it's folk.

What makes it art is the eye of the beholder and its celebration after. The pattern of light on a wall in that case would qualify and a habit of speech is found art. Who's going to say that anything cannot be art? So while art is for the peoples' sake, it is always also for its own sake. But to be folk you have to do it yourself and to apply some rigor, it has to be done the way they used to do it. Pegged joints, real butter, hand stitching and in the rare air, sonnets are folk art. What used to be disdained is now bought up wholesale. The appeal is because it's one of a kind. They didn't make folk art only because they needed to. They needed to and they made it because it expressed their love, their joy, their grasp of the beauty of life.

What's the difference between folk art and fine art except expertise and volume? Richard E. Wentz, founder of the religion department at ASU, proposes new categories of folk religion, folk spirituality, folk hierophants, folk poets, folk stories, folk preachers, but folk is as the folk does. There are folk critics too, meaning of the folk themselves, and folk intellectuals, which is the point of this diversion.

The trouble is that folk texts don't exist any more. Folk speech is oral not written. When a Mennonite gave a sermon if he wrote it out ahead he would be blamed for pride. He could read other's published sermons, but his own speaking was extemporaneous. Given the highly oral nature of folk religion, the transience of folk artifacts, what philosophical glue held the folk together?

Boehme

Jakob Boehme (1575-1624), itinerant shoemaker, philosopher of the *Ungrund* (unground), ground without a ground, refutes the charge that Pennsylvania German folk art is not founded on aesthetic principles in themselves. Boehme is the perfect philosophical origin for folk forms created by generations who spoke only German but lived in Pennsylvania. Böhme wrote his first book, *Die Morgenroete im Aufgang* especially in the folk process, for himself, and did not complete it. A manuscript copy of the unfinished *Aurora* of the spiritual structure of the universe reflected in sunlight in a dish was copied and made known.

It has always been the rap against the Dutch that they were uneducated, but Boehme, early translated into English by Sparrow starting 1635 and Law in 1764, had influences among the educated all over the place, no recommendation really to be followed by Milton, Blake, Coleridge, Yeats, and Gurdjieff, more a testament of corruption. If it complicated the folk they reveled in it to a degree, so nobility boasted they were folk who resisted learning even while faulting themselves for not having it and then having it.

Boehme had no education, was merely a shoemaker with visions, but "one of the most remarkable untrained minds," which shoemaker was like the baker, Conrad Beissel, founder of Ephrata. Should we not close Harvard so more could be untrained farmers and peasants in the Dutch artifact of original folk thought? The educated classes didn't want to share their originality with bumpkins but the bumpkins invented transcendentalism in America. Edwards and Emerson are not to be uttered in the same breath with these. What does it matter if Emerson's transcendentalism was preceded a hundred years, that "Pennsylvania German transcendentalism was healthy and living long before the Yankees in New England imported it second-hand from German Romanticism in the nineteenth century" (Stoudt, xix).

These folk turned a blind eye to the Puritans. Didn't much read them. Didn't much read English. The English retaliated by never reading the Germans, until they fell to Goethe, Rilke. The ultimate rejection, the folk went on their way as ever, making and doing, doing and making. In all these generations it was inevitable that some gain occurred, for the folk love the folk. Families loved families, mothers and fathers and children cooperated together. Gradually the trunks filled. Some blessed cases and chests entered the 21st century whole.

Folk Artist

The folk mother is not in commercial production. She makes things for her family, does her own cooking, cleaning, gardening. All the things modern marketing and science seek to deliver her from she does. Folk art among all peoples is domestic in intent. The best things done by the Navajo are for the home. Anna Mack was one of these. And when her daughter Florence wrote a groundbreaking master's thesis it was of *finding the home within*. So Anna's creations are folk mainstream, remnants of which begin to occur late 20th century.

She didn't make quilts for sale at markets or exhibitions. She made them for herself, her husband and children. They all had their own quilts. She left no specific embroidery show towels and Elisabeth Bechtel has only one remain, and that just with her initials. Kate Rosenberger's family left many examples. Anna made all her own clothes and left behind a plain Mennonite dress and bonnet that fits a very slender figure, a girl of 17 perhaps, her first communion dress. A fabulous example. She did her own cooking, which like the quilts and the dresses, was prepared according to her own standards, each dish with its own flair of perfection, her own take, an interpretation.

Curator

A second quality almost always true in families is that they repose the folk artists who preceded them. These curators hold collections of things as part of the tradition. Women pass down samples of their work to each other and to the generations as folk art begins to accumulate. It wasn't always embroidery, sometimes it was furniture, or china or pottery or recipes, later it was trained untrained MDs and PhDs but it was always what somebody in their family made.

In Anna's curatorship museum pieces to be conserved were put in a drawer, and what a drawer, a handmade Berks County chest. So the folk artist accumulates an oeuvre and won't necessarily show it to you either. Her own pieces are in use all over the house. The handed down ones are put away. There is no celebration of any of it. It is accepted for what it is, although the pies and cakes and boned chicken and mashed potatoes and doughnuts, the candied carrots and coffee are praised, the puddings and the shoofly pie, are, their appeal is immediate.

All the domestic arts are folk arts and all the moderns who seek to escape them for some mass produced imitation are doing just that. Prove this wrong, go singe a chicken. This makes the real folk art that remains, but somehow gets to market, worth a lot. Like even the lumber of their barns, any piece of country furniture, a cabinet make by a farmer to put cow medicine in is valuable, suited to placement in Scottsdale and Santa Monica for that country look.

The greatest problem of the folk is the compromise that interrupts the formation of the authorities, historical identity in families, the warps, whether we refer to the loss of historical faith, the loss of values or the right acting that grandma held. Identity gathering and modeling of on-line generations redefines the making of values and friendships. Even courtship can be essentially outside of folk time and place. Particular beliefs once held in families become negotiable. Family authorities cease.

Family expectations are not an issue. You can pretend to agree, if you must see them at all, then go back to chat with your new friends, peers who indeed have much to say in defining your identity. To them you say what you really think, but of course it is and must be only a mirror of what they think. They aren't grandma. Thus multiple generations of held beliefs, historical indeed, are rejected for contemporary make believe, fantasy. How stable will a generation that began in 1995 be? Will there be a turning toward the historical? Families are nothing if not historical.

Defolking The Denial of History

A lot of the pseudonymous and anonymous internet identities label themselves agnostics to communicate with each other, share criticisms of their mothers and fathers and carefully and carelessly misstate the selected facts of their lives and achievements to make themselves look good.

The defolked son or daughter may arrogate to themselves a gift from a parent or help from a relative. All of us have said and done this one way or another perhaps, but it was in private or to some friend or shouted midnight at the moon, not broadcast under a false name to gain recognition. This species of youth reject that folk stuff as superstition, incline maybe to a view that being is the unground of the internet, artificial intelligence. Maybe a cow is not really a cow at all, but where does milk come from?

Of course it is not possible to entirely escape the historical, there being a fixed aspect to gravity too. Identity anyway in youth is mythological, puts on all sorts of disguises until it finally sheds them for the historical one, which is merely saying your own name, that and when you have your own family you will take it up.

Alan Watts: A History of Fantasy, A Fantasy of History

There is no easy answer to the charge the folk are outdated, their values obsolete. They are. The folk teach their sons to respect their elders. This means to respect all the past, anything older than you. That makes them outdated. To the folk this respect is just common sense. The boundaries along the field; respect them and they respect you. The old burial ground on the hill, respect that. And if you don't the folk will never forget it. Hundreds of years later they will say your ancestor plowed up that cemetery. Respect your mother because she's older than you. Respect her, she is the first principle of your life. It is respect for yourself.

The debate between past and present comes down to a contest of history vs. re-history, or maybe to a debunking present it is de-history. The denial of the validity of the folk identity leads even to a doubt of empiricism.

Alan Watts has a credible take on historicity that springs from his respect for the ancient text, respecting elders again. His feeling for Lao-tzu makes him refute the notion that the *Tao Te Ching* "is a compilation of Taoist sayings by several hands. When I consider the confused opinions arising from textual criticism of the New Testament, I am in some doubt as to how seriously this debunking of the Lao-tzu legend should be taken. Since the latter years of the 19th century, scholars of the Western tradition, including many Chinese and Japanese, seem to have established a trend for casting doubt on the historicity of 'legendary' figures of the past-especially if they are of the religious or spiritual type. To please their professors, many successful graduate students affect peppery skepticism and an aura of scientific objectivity as a matter of protocol in submitting acceptable dissertations" (xxiii).

He "wonders whether pedants miss features which are obvious to the naked eye." "To me, the Tao Te Ching, the "Book of the Way and Its Power," could very obviously be the work of one hand, allowing for minor interpolations and for such inconsistencies, real or apparent, as may be found in the work of almost any philosopher. (xxiv)."

This "work of one hand" is a powerful respect of the elder, deducing unity and creative power where there is such. This is to say nothing of the possible inconsistencies that skeptics allege they have found from the single hands of other poets. The authorship of the Psalms, of the Iliad and Odyssey, have suffered quaint reductions or expansions under the multiple hands of critics who think editors wrote serially, but out of order, so that other editors had to put them in their real order, that is, clumped together thematically to please an editor's mind.

Stretching the Original

This issue impacts all ancient authorities to some extent. Taliesin was rewritten in the 14th century. In a way these are forgeries, but in another a homage to the 6th century. In some sense you could say Tolkien rewrote the Eddas and the sagas with also the 6th century Anglo Saxon, but that shows the point. If you stretch the concept of original into being infinitely plastic then even fanzines of Tolkien, even slash fiction where two characters have dialogue and experiences never dreamed of by Tolkien could be considered in the spectrum of its originals' authorship, absurd as it sounds. It matters not the slightest that this would horrify Tolkien as much as Satan's herohood would Milton. Tolkien would probably file some suit under patent law.

This infinitely plastic spectrum of stretching the original is a lot like Ignatius Donnelly foisting his Atlantis upon Plato, or any fiction writer claiming to have discovered a notebook, a ms. of Sappho, the Pope, any figure, Lincoln, that shows he or she did not do either what they said or you thought or what records say. Everything is counterfeit except the rewrite. These fictional deeds are never of light, but always dark.

They are not ballyhooing Blake and his wife praying to the Holy Ghost for guidance, as they often did, or his call in the start of *Jerusalem,* "I also hope the Reader will be with me, wholly One in Jesus our Lord, who is the God [of Fire] and Lord [of Love] to whom the Ancients look'd and saw his day afar off, with trembling & amazement." The rewrites appeal to the morbid sensibility nurtured by lust, war and apocalypse. Imagine reversing this scenario, finding heroes among the goats, nobility among the peasants.

It is unclear how many times the original elders have been stretched to their own defamation for purposes of fame or fortune. Mythmaking pretends to revise history or originate history. It is called a *History of Middle Earth*, but it is also called *A Brief History of Time,* as well as a *History of England.* But the idea of history, with its versions and interpretations, when applied to mythology is completely fantastic. In these second versions, Socrates never died from hemlock. He died certainly, but how do you like, captured by aliens, left a double in his place, was really a Jew, went to the Himalayas, or he was just an invention of Plato and never existed. None of it occurred? The one that has had this most systemically done is Jesus.

Freud doubted Moses was in Egypt. Form critics doubted Moses wrote at all. In this plastic mindset it is probable to hear anything, isn't that what freedom of speech is all about, say anything, say Moses was never in the Bible and have it believed on television, just as you can believe that there were women writers of the Bible on the internet. There is good currency in debunking the past and in reaffirming it. So Troy was both an invention and an archaeological dig. You can have your cake and eat it to.

There are many distinguished forgers: Heinrich Schliemann, hero of archeology, used the Iliad to find his Troy. The Troy he thought he found was not the Troy that Troy had been, it was actually layer vii a, but it was good enough for Schliemann to become both a smuggler and forger of "King Priam's Treasure." T. J. Wise, legitimate bibliographer of Shelley, Browning, Tennyson, etc. found business so good he not only catalogued, he forged the originals too. Good men all theirs was a commercial venture for fame and fortune for retelling.

Some of this can be beautiful. Retelling is a doctrine of classicism. *Paradise Lost* is a retelling. *The Aeneid* is a retelling, *The Illiad* is a retelling of a history of the war, but if the work is fictional that does not mean that the author is too. In mistaking the author for the genre lots of peppery grads have gone agog. They are virtual poets, but look like, act like and talk like scholars. The trouble is that poets are really editors according to this phenomena and editors are forgers. Harvard run amuck.

The invention of history and the inventions of higher criticism move the boundary stones so far they form a tautology out of the "one hand." The fact, the history, the poet's telling, subsequent retellings, the editing, the demythologizing, the editor, the forger, the poet. The only thing left out is the fact. We are short on facts, hardly believe in contexts. When the empirical is lost and the empire of the real subverted we can all go around to quote

Prufrock in as many ways as we can and his speech rhythms will be art.

Folk Take

The folk have a take on all this, what's the good of it to the living? What kind of lives did these fictionalizers live? To the folk an artist's life justifies his work not his work his life. They think it better to submerge themselves in the fields, forges, kitchens and barns and serve out their time in service and duty to others, not to push themselves to the front. The folk measure of a poet is how did he live, how die. Was he faithful, hard working. Practically none of this matters to the elite who willingly sacrifice their children, family and home for their faux work. The folk live among their children, die there of old age and its causes, not of despondency.

Taking Down Buddha

The problem of stretching the original is that it does not save the past even if it celebrates it some way or other. There is a better argument that stretching the elder demolishes the past. Tolkien vii a will be excavated someday by a new Schliemann who will sell hobbit paraphernalia, but the original hobbit will be buried far beneath. This was the 7th version of the original. Is this idea too fictional for his fans?

If you think it impossible that Tolkien could be lost maybe you think the feeble structures around you are permanent. But home, school, car are all piles of rubble waiting to be a stone, plastic, steel midden of lives. Cannot Tolkien go the way of the Bible, which has been stretched and misshapen by so many critics? The supernatural is the proper realm of fantasy and sci fi, but the Testaments are always supernatural. They have been explained away. This has been artfully done.

To take down any renowned artifact takes some doing. Western demolition teams are jealous of the Taliban because they had such an easy time to dynamite the Buddhas. You can demo the outer, but demoing the inner takes more time. Alan Watts complains that once they got going on the Testaments they kept going on all the other ancient works too of the "religious and spiritual type." In their place they erect what dramas, fantasies of themselves?

Demolition reinterprets by fantasy. A boy reading that he is a folk product, a weft upon the reinforced strand in families of fathers and mothers will construe this to mean they are the primordial yab/yum, thus turning real persons into mere abstractions. These boys have gone around impersonating folk of other cultures for centuries now. They go to the Ganges to be Indians, to Fargo to be Indians, they go everywhere from the rain forest to the steppes. But everybody there sees them as outsiders, not a member of the folk. The good news is that they are unbelievably members of the folk too.

Taking Down The Tree

Anybody can take down their tree, mistreat their dog. Early settlers planted Aleppo Pines in some neighborhoods in the Sonoran desert, 80 to 100 years ago. The Homestead Neighborhood for several blocks along Pinchot in Phoenix is lined on both sides with these giants 60 to 80 feet high, desirable for cooling, birds, scent and ambiance, while further south we must be content with the Ironwood of 1500 years. There are some Aleppos in other neighborhoods too, but not planted together. They tower over the mulberry and chinaberry. Down the street a new neighbor takes down his Aleppo.

No reason. Why do people mistreat dogs? The cause isn't in the trees but in ourselves. It was big, but half gone when noticed. What could have been done, shoot the guy? Ransom the tree? Call the city? Futile. We loaded a pickup with three trips of sectioned trunk and hauled them to a back yard. It will not revive from these "cuttings." Forty feet of trunk remained standing. Next morning there was a stump. The severed limbs lined the curb as a kind of wood fence. Some of the sections split and hollowed now make homes in backyards for desert tortoises. The rest tilt at odd angles like gravestones. Aneirin: "whose grave is this, this one and this? Ask me I know them."

This is a parable, a lament for all lost species? The Branch. Which do you miss most, what you have never seen, hillsides inundated with robins, Glen Canyon? The light shining from the herb in Isaiah? If we care, and the list could be long, then we should care about this tree too. One generation could lay it all down. It helps to understand Andrew Mack's saying, "if they do this in a green tree, what shall they do in a dry?"

Fact As Artifact

Saving the past means conservation of the fact as artifact. If you change the surface, reduce, remove the patina you destroy the fact. That facts are like artifacts is evident from this. The Genesis account, et. al. needs to held in a factual state, in the dark, away from the showbiz lights, to preserve it, just like any painting. Facts like artifacts need to be protected from the UV, acidic airs, the dust and soot of intellectual commerce. But the dealers like the literary critics have cut down the highboys to fit low ceilinged homes, cut down high pieces to their idea of proper size to fit décor to sell them better. They have married pieces they considered alike to fit mutual defects, but not accurately together, for they aren't experts, but they can fool the buyer.

Refinishing the Classics

The classics are like an old oak table, pitted and scarred with cigarette burns that you think should be refinished, taking it down to the bare wood, if need be taking it to a factory to be plane sanded. Just refinish the top. Bare wooding the classics, Socrates is less and less a man and more and more an allegory of Plato. Refinished how many times? Minute crinkling in the varnish of the original, the imperfections of use, rounded edges, white wood worn in drawers, do not prove the original a fake.

Literary critics and forgers have cut down the masterpieces, falsely wedded them, making them forgeries of themselves. Forgeries hardly seems accurate, fiveries, sixeries. How much difference is there between amputating a Chippendale, the Taliban blowing up the Afgan Buddhas and the critics arguing Satan the hero of *Paradise Lost*? Oh but that was Blake, he gets an exemption. He was all peppery about Milton.

Question: What happened when people got all peppery about Blake?

Answer: He gouged his plate!

There is so much revisionism going on one might think none of the revered classical writers and their texts are what they said they were or seemed to be. But in fact, if fact exists, this is true only of the revisionists and by this we more and more mean the extreme biologists who cut and paste. They are not what they seem to be.

Grandma's Folk ID

A very large part of folkhood is the way each family holds itself together, preserves its history, traditions and unity, even while changing. In a family such as our case here, which shows dramatic evidence of preservation of artifacts over two centuries, each generation had anchors, who played the glue, not just in the sense of preservation, but in preserving the authority, past and present, of what constitutes right and wrong. This sums up in one word, grandma. Whatever interferes with this transmission of right and wrong erodes the folk. The message of the folk is that they continue in sameness, a kind of vulgarity like the earth itself. The earth is not so glorious as idealists picture. The earth is dirt and storm, drought and flood, but continues its extremes because it is what it is.

Civilizations, peoples, families, tribes contain all these extremities coupled with identity. When the identity of a tribe dissipates the tribe dies out. Ask Ishi, the last Yahi, ask the Mohicans. Any attempt to preserve the tribe against the forces of the media makes the elders seem reactionary. Unmodern. Uninformed. Ignorant. Only conservatives believe in the single text! The outdated one hand! As the children age, if they are lucky, they have a chance to become elders, if the tribe, family survives. What do the Hopi elders want more than anything but for the youth to speak Hopi, live Hopi, respect authority, practice Hopi, love Hopi. All this is for its own sake, so the Hopi survive. In the same manner each family with an identity wants to survive.

The PA Germans stopped speaking German, their youth especially, because the benefits were great. Still there are enclaves where the language is spoken. There are corresponding authorities in these families to those in the tribes, if the families yet survive. They set the boundaries. There is a religion also that to the instant internet culture is as quaint as that of the Hopi. If the family flourishes, bits and pieces come down, artifacts, but more importantly ideas, stories, visits, memories, letters, calls, prayers, anguish. This is the glue that holds together the inheritance. Memories must call from out the deep before you turn again home. And when you come home what do you find, the rubble of time and space or the order preserved until you could occupy the ground? It probably means you have to give up your childishness and anger and to some extent your ego before you can put on the mantle designed for you. How can you, who were all your life a swan, capable of such grace and carriage, such beauty and purity, how can you settle for being accepted among ducks?

The internet replaces family with friends, people who agree for those who demand you keep the boundaries. The tribes and families are the true human diversity. Those who claim diversity values for themselves seek to equivocate these values into mass movements, suitable to some idea of a global democracy. Democracy as long as they rule. Just like the English.

Who doesn't want to hear again how the Mennonites were capable of a cure in their broad appeal for the rights of others not specifically Mennonites. **The first question** of *Conversation* takes reason to task among bloggers, forgers, editors, liars, sinners, in fact, to all men and women and all of nature and humanity:

Question two is, "Are there also those who are not conscious of possessing a higher spirit than brutes, and yet maintain, that they can keep their minds in a good state of rest in this life."

Answer: "whenever any of these become of another and a better mind, and get into other reflections, (which cannot take place, however, without divine agency) and continue in them,--they will come not only to a knowledge of the nature of their condition, but also to a knowledge of themselves, and their higher spirit.

Question three is: "in what then, does one's true knowledge consist?

Answer: This knowledge consists in two things; 1. to know that of and from the self there is no power to do or understand any thing, either in matters external or spiritual, 2. To have a knowledge of this transitory and troublesome state of life" (5-6).

Works Cited

Christian Spiritual Conversation. Lancaster, PA: John Baer's Sons, 1892.

Don Dedera. *Navajo Rugs.* Flagstaff, Northland Press. 1975.

Freud. *Moses and Monotheism.*

Stephen W. Hawking. *A Brief History Of Time.* NY: Bantam, 1988

Henry J. Kauffman. *Pennsylvania Dutch American Folk Art.* NY: Dover, 1964.

Rufus Jones. Preface to John Joseph Stroudt. Jacob Boehme's *The Way to Christ in Modern Translation.*

John Joseph Stoudt. *Pennsylvania German Folk Art.* Allentown, PA: Schlechter's, 1966

Alan Watts. Tao: The Watercourse Way. NY: Pantheon Books, 197.

A Day in the Life

*In The Consolation of Philosophy, a conversation between
Boethius and a female personification of philosophy, the Roman
consul executed by Emperor Theodoric in 524 wrote from prison the
last year of his life, "no one can ever truly be secure until he has
been forsaken by Fortune."*

Conversations with her those last four years by phone did not
answer all the questions, but the talk was wide ranging, facetious and
serious.

Writing on both sides fast to get the rapid fire cadence, I
scrawl details and put them in a folder. The notes could be cryptic
and illegible. Scraps became full sheets. Sometimes I would type
them immediately, but sometimes months went by and the thread
was lost except for the direct quotes. I had no intention to produce
this *Libby*.

She was lonely, living alone with that recuperated hip and
repaired cataract that restored her sight. Sometimes she would
poormouth to bait me. So I would tease her.

Do you want me to come out there and take care of you?

I had actually tried to send my daughter in this behalf after
her hip broke, but that plan was rejected.

"Everybody," she said, "wants to take care of me."

Her brother left her a legacy in his life insurance when he
died. My older, now deceased brother, said he would take care of

her. Her sister, also deceased, said she would take care of her! Nobody seemed to think her competent. Once I asked whether if she needed money she would feel free to ask me for it. She said yes! That was the best part of talking to her, the remarks, the jokes, the pure sarcastic puns. She had 12,000 shares of Sara Lee.

The Humor of Defect

Her wit was more deeply etched by the social deterioration of age. She was still mobile when her peers had fallen. Cicero thinks an irascible nature will out at any age, that the best way to endure old age is to practice the cardinal virtues. But the practice of virtue is dangerous.

Humor is the celebration of defect. Moral turpitude makes us laugh, briefly makes us whole at the defect's expense. Wit, no cosmetic effort of beauty, made her whole, translated the antimonies into light. These witticisms could be serious, farcical or in between, depending on the flow, but the semblances of dialogue, mostly facetious, were always played to her trump card. What else did she have to do anyway than exchange lighthearted confidences by phone. I liked to get her when she was in the basement doing the wash or folding the clothes, that usually seemed to amuse her.

Abraham: A Day in The Life

One time she cornered me into debating the Hebrew idea of a day, as if it were a symbol for her predicament of age. The Pennsylvania Dutch are born chiliasts, meaning they believe in the idea of a thousand year period variously applied and have for hundreds of years. She took up the day/age theory with a vengeance in reference to Abraham and realism, defined by what she could see, determined what she would believe. A good realist declines the view that all the really good things are invisible, that's for Wittgenstein, that's for romantics. She and her mother had a lot in common, but

Anna was a born romantic, so naturally she gave birth to Elizabeth the realist. Debate between these two never occurred. Debate was saved to put in order the universe of untutored males.

Abraham was old and shriveled when he was promised a progeny as numerous as the sands of the sea. That was against realism. Nowadays we would say "contemplate yourself surrounded by what you need in order to succeed." But this realist wanted no reconciliation of the real with the invisible, argued that days were different in Abraham's day, that a year then was measured differently. Presumably a lot shorter. To the counter that she seemed to believe Abraham mythological not real she stamped her foot. "I'm too tired to think," she said.

Of Abraham's age and more I urge: "Did not the Gardener say that if you have faith as a grain of mustard seed and say to the mountain move, it will be carried into the sea?"

Yes, she replied, "but that doesn't mean faith in yourself," meaning, "you male egotists mistake your own ego for God."

The glory of her wit was not only that it got over into phenomenology, it made her adept at categorical denial and affirmation. Referring to this manuscript, she tells nephew Robert. "He is keeping me alive," meaning these drafts now circulating are making her the center of attention and that she is being celebrated so much she feels like maybe she will put off being terminal a while yet to enjoy it. Many people reach their 90's with failing memory and incapacity of higher thought just when they have something to say. Puissant at 94, her humor is ironic and dry. It is a beautiful defect.

She calls it, "making a remark."

Acme

On a shop, trying to get some kosher grape out of Acme, as if she were preparing a Seder, it being near Passover, but not finding any, she accosts the kosher foods clerk, "I guess I won't write a letter of protest about anti-Semitism here."

The lady is affronted, "are you accusing me of anti-Semitism?"
"No," she says, deadpan, "Acme."

She does it for fun. What can anybody do to an old lady?

Good sense of humor is a sign of intelligence.

"I didn't know that."

Dry.

Still, for all that, not much of a drinker. Has to remind herself to drink. Likes juices though, as long as they're pure.

This satiric bent is nurtured by history, travel, literature and a thirst for experience that in the next breath is denied. It is a satiric realism. Questioned, it takes umbrage.

She can't write anymore, never showed her true colors on paper anyway, such good proper sentences. This is a habit of the clandestine mind; don't leave a record. Protect yourself in print.

But she could make a remark like a bee sting.

Cartilage

She has reminded me twice by phone in the last weeks of an occasion when I had the cartilage out of my knee in 1964, that is, the old way with the six inch cut. She remarks that after she and her sister visited in the hospital they had a good laugh in the parking lot over their nephew's "pain."

Is that in the medium sarcastic range?

Ophelia

"I'm up to surviving" she says, as if in the middle of some book. Specifically Jerry and Dayle, her older stepson, with his fiancée, are in town to announce their engagement and are to be married at Media Presbyterian in May, the third time.

"Will they marry anybody!"

When the church administrator gave them a booklet he was asked, as a favor to the First Female Elder, that being, herself, which minister, Don Norquist or Bob Keissel (who married Lib and Marvin) would marry them. She considered the whole, "cheeky."

So May 15 at 11 AM to townhouse for lunch with the bride we go. The bride has a girlfriend from VA, got the wedding package. Already had her dress. Then they went up to Allentown, Marvin's boyhood home, to a farmer's market and got dry corn. You soak it, bake it, boil it like stew. They also got the farmer's cheese, but "not original," wrapped in cellophane. The commercial cheese. It was a big social calendar that Sunday, birthday party for Bud, then Jerry's wedding, unless my notes are garbled. How could you do both in a day? The bride in her 60's wore short white hair, a long pale pink chiffon gown with ruffles at the bottom and plastic ribbons trailing down the back with a wreath on her head.

"I keep calling her Ophelia," she says.

"I'm nasty, really nasty."

My wife had rescued a half dead kitten from the alley in the hot May heat, but I don't want a cat. I raise chows.

She remembers how my brother had been so proud of Bingo, a cat of the family's youth, exclaimed to her, "isn't she beautiful." Being then good, she only smiled.
Now she says, "Ophelia's a good name for your kitten."

She revved out Shakespeare then and together we pursued the Ophelia menace. She tortured me with Polonius' advice to Laertes, Ophelia and her flowers, rosemary and pansies.

I keep thinking, "mummery," but suppress it for, "wall!"

This led to Morley's "Travels in Philadelphia," and his preface to Shakespeare.
Her vision of the world as foible and vanity these quips compel.

Balaam

Another time I tried to differentiate by phone the apparent initial English "L" from the actual "C' in the German cursive handwriting of her great grandfather Bechtel.

Jokingly upon the difficulty of German to an untutored eye such as my own, as well as upon the guttural sounds, which however can be understood if you sound them out, I mentioned that I had, in a story, put a putative German into the mouths of mules bearing their patrons to the bottom of the Grand Canyon, but that this pidgin would surely offend her.

"Who knows why mules should speak German," I baited her. "Their language is too gross for your eye."

"Not at all." she said, "I don't care, mules aren't Arabian Horses. Of course they speak poorly."

"Maybe they spoke Pennsylvania Dutch."

She countered, "maybe that's what Balaam's Ass spoke." (BALALABAMM! Seeing the Angel Poet." *Gobbet*, Feb. 2011)

"But that was English!"

One or the other of us wondered what Balaam's Ass had actually said in Hebrew. Then Maimonides (III, 99) got targeted for exposing the oppositions of Hebrew homonyms. When the angel was speaking for the ass it was good, "the Lord opened the ass's mouth." But when the angel was adversarial, "I have come here to oppose you," it was bad. Not that this resembled the diction of my poor plebes who said:

Mine vurst vessel,
mine strubal vagen,
be smirchen sie hovel,

bestrudal mine bier kanne."

"Well." she says, "I don't know that mules spoke vurst"
("This Meing, Mooing, Mewingmuling Song, " *elimae 2006).*

"Yes, it is a living wurst."

So we tampered with the English, German, Hebrew,
Pennsylvania Dutch ass.

I confided I had made my wife study Hebrew for just such
occasions. We parted amicably. An airplane speaking as it were of a
spaceship, she said that of course my wife could learn any such
thing.

Matzo

This is not to say there was no return fire. Al Creamer, her
boyfriend at the time her father died prematurely in 1927, sent her 17
yellow roses for her birthday (how, she wonders, did he remember
yellow?). She, grieving her father, didn't respond for three days.
Now, 75 years later, she feels bad about it. Laugh if you want, she's
serious.
How could he afford it she says, his parents weren't rich.

I think to myself, "maybe he loved you!"

On this terminable death voyage she has confided during a
visit from Robert and Cynthia that she may have loved a Russian
émigré artist who boarded with the family after her father died. This
Russian did a bust of her, which she has never bothered to mention.
Her interest died when she found he talked to other girls. Realist
opaque. Then the repartee went something like this:

What did you have for dinner last night?

"Hot dogs."

Beef?

"No."

Turkey?

No. "Pork dogs. Meat wieners."
She relishes the Anglo-Saxon as though it were food.

I tell her my wife won't cook pork, but recall the sauerkraut browned around a roast that my mother cooked, recipe via Anna.

She remembers the smoked tongue around Memorial Day. Now, she says, you probably can't buy it. It goes into dog food. She's living high off the hog.

Then rapid fire: "so you never found a boy who loved you!"

She: "I like matzo crackers."

Then, "what. . .?"

"You're a matzo Mennonite!"

She ends the call with, "I think we talk too much." I see what she means in retrospect.

McHusband and McWife

Years before, she remembers, her sister came home once from holiday at the last leaf cleanup of the year. Heavy rain and wind had made the huge sycamore leaves disappear from the tree.

It was while raking these leaves years later, at age 72 that she says God told her to marry Marvin.

It's hard to know what she means by that, whether face value or some witticism. Now she cannot rake at all. Instead she just finished the questionnaire from Friends Life Care. It is the age of feedback, yea or nay don't fit in the form. Maybe it's the same answer she gives to the do-gooder who asks how she's doing.

She wants to query them, "well how do you think I'm doing?"

Cooped up, bunged up, stirs the nasty. Satire fires off the port bow:
"I'm rolling down the hill trying to keep my head above water."

What do sycophants say to that?

But now she's rolling.

"They live a vulgarity, got a Mc Job, a Mc Husband or a Mc Wife."

Old women rock and roll?

There's punch in the bowl.

Let's talk about the weather.

She says society is vulgar. Critiques the dance of Brittany and her girls at the Super Bowl halftime as marionettes, factory girls doing a space dance in a clone suit. They probably won't survive the alternative future.

I offer the male code to restore polite society. Vigilantism gets her back up, malefactors corrected and punished by other men, but outside the law. Well, will women do it?

"It sounds just horrible."

"What is the code? The unwritten code?"

I'm not going to write it down if you don't know it.

He's such a nice boy.

Many Subjects

There are many subjects in her mind and conversations.

Do you want spiritual authenticity, a sense of community?

Do you want to hear about Mennonites?

Man, who doesn't?

There is a series of black and white photos of her after dinner, age 92, November 2002. In only two of them is she serious. Her head is elevated in laughter. Eyes look up at the ceiling.
How does this lead to milk cows and that Anna's father, Henry Mack, remarried when Anna was 8?

Of her own mother, "she spoiled me rotten."

At the time I interpreted these swift changes of direction as a bit of spirit, meaning she was recouping from her sadness at husband Marvin's passing, the year before, April 20, 2001.

She quarrels with my reference to the Henry Mack/Lizzie Bechtel love story as an appeal to the feminine side! Says that's out of date.

The last time we talked she ended with "well, I guess we could talk forever."

Forever and a day.

Dogged

Speaking of marriage, until 50 she wanted a dog, a dachshund she says. She lived with her mother though, who, being raised on the farm had had too many dogs. In those years from 30 to 60 she worked 7 AM until 9 PM on weekends, almost as long during the week.

When she was 60, and her mother had died she thought about getting a dog, but decided it would be too much trouble, tie her down from her travels what with the vet and the boarding.

So at 72 she got married! Fired out the announcement with ferocity.

She perches on the couch, knees together, a brilliantly superior smile on her face and looked way down the nose: "guess what I'm going to do?"

Remark-making can dog anyone who has been taken more seriously than they deserve. Once, after announcing to the dissolute Tom Whitbread at a party, "I'm a Republican!" He crowed: "you have a fine mind!"

The clerk at the library said, "God knows we need the rain."
"Well, God would know that wouldn't He."

I'm shopping early, it is almost April, '04.
What do you want for your birthday?
"Nothing. Wait till I'm 95, and have something to celebrate."

Visited by the parish nurse, the Saints Alive leader, official maiden ladies who say to her, I love your mind, which is all anybody has, she threatens to start keeping a diary, a record of "old age." She doesn't know this record of her thoughts and moods exists. I haven't told her on purpose. Imagine how it would be if somebody were to write down every word you said in jest, take it seriously and turn it into fodder for geese?

I do tell her though after she is hospitalized and send her an early draft.

How did Dr. Johnson feel with Boswell writing it all down?

They tell her, "I love your mind."

In the context of everyday ministries among the old that's about like saying she can read a tinfoil candy wrapper, not admit in the middle of inquisitions she never understood Kierkegaard.

What's the mental capacity of an elder in the homes but a mass of prejudice and selfishness uttered in choruses of moans in front of the TV, "help me, help me?" Yes, I have seen it.

I love her mind too though, but it's not as if she thinks this means let's you and me talk about your grandchildren.

"I'm a loner" she confesses.

"I'm so glad."

Everybody is alone all the time. To prove it I have mailed her a 75 cent copy of Malamud's, *The Fixer*. Saul Bellow contrives to die the same week she does, as does the Pope.

I'm playing mixed doubles one day and parenthesize, you know mixed doubles is with women.

She says, "well I didn't think they mixed it up with horses!"

Starlings

There are 300 blackbirds in my birdbath screeching like grackles.

She says, "maybe they are starlings," which I now realize they are.

Wonderful name Star-lings.

What constellation are you from?

The City of Philadelphia wanted to control the unsanitary ways of the downtown starlings, but the uptown bird people were in uproar over poisoning them.

She says there were a lot of pigeons down at the RR station in Media but they're gone now.

I ask, are "you suggesting foul play."

She says, "I like that Andy."

Maybe it's vigilantes.

Men

There is a flood warning, fog and snow, trees are bending in the rain. She gets out Andrew's leaf that he gave her, which hangs in the kitchen now. But she is scheduled to receive a visit from a 96 year old admirer who is driving over to see her. She says maybe she should call and tell him not to come.

I say, "he'll be there."

He is the brother of Betty Wentz whose wife, of equal age, lives in Oregon where she is native.

I say, "men are capable of much devotion."

She replies, "men are capable of exceeding their capabilities."

Not a part of this world, my mistress. I would say sister but she had all the brother she could want. Her life has the current of sacrifice in it. She is combing her hair now because there is no appointment this week. No bald spot, but one bright spot, she got another box of fruit.

These boxes just appear from nowhere, left at the door, the delivery didn't even knock.
"It has a bell!"

"My hair has wings."
Einsteinian hair, she says; the TV shows would mistake her for an angel.

It's all relative she says, punning.

"If you're not persecuted you fall into apathy." She actually says that, stealing the line from the last chapter. Where could that have sprung from but the very apotheosis of Mennonite psychology? Wait and see.

The light-dark of these conversations will one moment pierce like levity, in another plop like a dark hat on your lap.

She is catholic about Lent, monks, penitentes, Ash Wednesday next week. Ambivalent friends at art school had to give up things like candy, but on St. Patrick's Day would eat back the candy they had given up. Rationality. St. Pat is not a saint anymore, she says, a liberator from Lent and fish on Friday (says her driver Lou). That doesn't come from God but from the Pope who wanted Italians to each fish to help the industry (and Mel?).

This season when you consider Christ's sacrifice make a sacrifice too, she says.

Speaking of cognates, Latin-taught grammar, crossword puzzles, French and Italian cognates, she says, brother Robert and I have opposite aims, but our children are similar.

Maybe our aims are not so different.

Reliving Anna's farm days again, fleeing the farm to get away from everything, the German language and the opinions, this liberation was a release from the past. Getting up to communion in Bally wasn't easy. Uncle Andrew Mack, the bishop, was older than Anna by two generations, but they shared mutual respect and affection, 34 to 80. But not a part of this world.

Icons and Hot Water Heaters

We dispute the semantics of "hot water heater." Marvin worked for a company that insisted that they be called simply water heaters. Isn't it as obvious as wrong in right that this is so? Marvin was astutely cynical about commerce, looked for investments that had a social good attached. His view was that it's just a matter of personality the way the rhetorical smirks of commerce and philosophy wage war against each other. Truth is hard to find and he would speculate it by the hour. Just take any affirmation you like. Why not just admit without dispute that "dust storms may exist," or that Abraham may be too old?

When I invoke the life of the mind in these and other matters to players at the tennis clinic they eye me like fearful bovines.

The Greek orthodox don't worship icons, that is, the representations of dead saints.

Her contention is, "I'm not an icon cause I'm not dead!"
I want to tease, "but you will be!"

Which of course would generate, "which, an icon or dead?"

Boundary

I can have these conversations with her in my mind now. She
doesn't even have to be there. But she is. Or she was. Or she still is.
It seems to depend on your point of view whether when you walk in
the dark before dawn you pass through hundreds of years of history
that at any particular time might be living or dead. And getting the
last laugh too. Let's see, is that an icon? No.

A myth?

No.

She is a boundary I patrol to confirm the fences, to see that
all is sound, safe in the camp.

On diagnosing Alzheimer's: there's no test in the brain of a
live person for which there is an incremental diagnosis,
500x5000x500000. Also that there's some chemically directed
treatment put into the brain that takes the disease out. The long
progression of the disease and the upset at the denial in society
makes this Alzheimers of families so.

Somehow we get to my recommendation that they put her
picture in the window of her bank, which has a teller in her 80's,
because "banks are people too."

But she reminds me, "so are computers."

Mad At God

It becomes obvious how attractive she is to the opposite sex. When Marvin had begun to stir her, her main concern was not to hurt his feelings, for she intended to let him down. Raking her beloved Sycamore leaves in the context of having prayed about this dilemma got an answer.

But people are fickle. When she broke her hip she was "mad at God because I couldn't take care of myself" which really means that she couldn't take care of Marvin. So she took the tactic of acting as though it "wasn't so bad."

This defense threw Marvin off, gave him the wrong cues and because she didn't share the pain he thought she didn't have any. She surmises now that he was jealous, thought she was malingering, which, for his disease, Alzheimer's, made it more difficult for him. He knew he had Alzheimer's but was in denial too. Still withal, considering the ways over to the exit sign it could have been worse. He escaped with his gall bladder intact, no hepatitis from blood transfusion, no cirrhosis, no liver transplant, no 5 way heart. She has aspirin and Advil.

In all this her physical therapy for the hip is recommended to all infirm: step up, 1,2,3. Turn failure into success, weakness into strength, 1,2,3. All wanting "to exceed their capabilities."

Stepson Bruce finished radiation for brain cancer. His older son, 23, is in jail on murder charges. The State police questioned him and he reached for a gun in his belt. They wanted the gun because it had been matched for an unsolved murder. His bail is 100K. Five

police took him down. Bruce blames Judy. Judy blames Bruce.
Brian got the calaboose.

I can hear the metaphors ringing.

She's on a three month recall for eye cataract surgery but
when she gets tired from reading she uses liquid tears. There is an
eclipse of the moon tonight. The trees are late, the leaves not down.

I ask her, "you think I'm a good Mennonite for not voting?"

She responds, "Henry voted, but he was concerned about
Helen going out with a Democrat."

She has mailed great nephew Aaron a form to fill out. Check
the blanks:
The check I sent is:

1) never received it

2) lost it

3) won't cash it

4) can't go to the bank.

Followed by the query "whether you still use cash?"

She went to buy new orthopedic shoes and pulled out a check
to pay but was told, "we don't accept checks any more."

To her friend Bud on his birthday, "I'm here today to know
how to act when I get to be 97."

CEO

Realists are grieved by expressionists.

And it's so terrible to grow up when the realists come to get cha. Considering mutual dislike of the bourgeois, the drinks, the gossip and the social act I once thought I could have been her son. Before she was terminal, as she now boasts, she prattled of any silly thing in her life (not so easily the serious things, but they were left alone mostly), from George Eliot on TV to translations of Virgil.

Now, CEO of her own death, she has responsibilities, is often too busy to talk because there are these details to arrange. She dictates her dénouement. Sell the house. Sign the papers. Get the lists going. Are those letters of appreciation coming in. Entertain the guests at the bedside.

Under the influence of such "realism" I doubt a common philosophy, but then the image of her from childhood blinds my memory: Lady Philosophy. I'm like her father, sacrifice time, energy, will for duty. She would hate to call it love. She hated that Howard was so "dominated," assumes that I too think he was weak.

Actually I think, looking at his image, that he was tough. But appearances are deceiving. In all the years I made inquiries of her family, from the 1970's on, in all the 30 years after Anna died, she never mentioned the hoard of watercolors, the books, the documents, the files of evidence, barely spoke of the linens, the gaudy Dutch china. Her letters about the Mennonites in the late 80's were a partial exception, partial because a lot of it is public record. Now she is gone I get to divine who Grandmother Mack's grandmother was.

But the effervescence lasts.

She asks the church bus driver, Charlie, if he's going to wear his Santa Claus outfit this year. Biddies on the left and right think Charlie's going to drive up as Saint Nick.

But she buttons her realism at church, prudently at circle, Sunday School and study group when the ladies talk about the rapture. Mennonites are not utterly enraptured. She can wear the protective coloring of the flock very well. They see her as strait-laced and serious, a person who needs to be protected even while they are afraid of her. My siblings are. Who isn't?

It's no wonder she says that "they can't tell when I'm kidding and when I'm serious!"

I'm always kidding, so we get along.

But it's not all satire, there is a longer rhythm to her thought, a wisdom, perhaps a greater part reflection and concentration applied before she surrendered to the end game that preoccupies her.

Time's Up, A Day in The Life Of An Age

Marvin had two watches, but would come into the kitchen to look at the clock on the wall. She thought he was checking the time against his watch, told him to get it repaired. Now she realizes he looked at the clock in the kitchen because he couldn't process time, that is, as an abstraction. What the eyes saw the mind didn't. Seeing he did not see, so in spite of his watches he never knew what time it was.

Sight is another aspect to a day in the life of an age.

Among all the possible connections made in verbal jousting, connections joining cataracts, colors, time and memory, she fastens upon a vet who had treated a blind lizard. Diagnostic blood work found the two foot long lizard to be on the brink of diabetes because it had fat deposits behind the eyes which made it blind. The vet prescribed a daily walk for lizard and a diet. The treatment worked.

"Lizard receives sight," I want to holler, but it's not a miracle.

She now has her sight back after suffering that left eye a decade. She always said if she survived Marvin she would have it done, but couldn't risk it if she had him to care for. These days, when she goes to the hospitals, as patient, not visitor, spunky men as lean as posts comment about how she has kept her figure. Punning on her name, Young?

Going to get new glasses this Friday, she felt "divorced" from the old. Glasses are like husbands, she says.

She wears the old boys habitually in the kitchen to protect her eyes from the heat of the stove, the cold of the fridge. But the divorce caused a triangle. "My blind eye seems to be jealous. I 'm used to doing everything on the left side (the repaired eye) but now the right eye (the blind one) wants to pull me back so I use both eyes. It wants to see too!" She had had the habit of turning her head to make contact with images; now the right eye wants to straighten the head.

As if reading this as a paper submitted to some convention she concludes, "so it's not only what you see, it's what your brain interprets about what it sees."

But if it were a poem it would read:

If vision is so mental dear,

what shall we say of ears?

There's just no telling what when you get up in the morning of your last day and you're still alive. It's that long, the afterlife.

After the husbands, the cataracts, the glasses, while there's still no end of tests a doctor gives with gadgets and of none of these disasters can you read a week later, would you say you have no other good eye to see with while the surgery heals? Does that mean you are afraid?

No, angry is more like it.

"My eye tells me how long I can read," she says, "even large print. "The brain gets upset because it thinks since I have sight in one eye I can see better, but I can't, I have to be careful. I get this push once in a while to do something I can't do, neither impulse nor irrational, a sympathetic nervous system thing between the right eye and left, as if the right eye could affect the left eye." The two eyes were designed to work together.

"I practice by shooting used tissues in the wastebasket from close range. And I miss!"

Make-Believe Life

There are other daily tests too, Tiggy, her nursing student driver, quit or was fired today,

"I yelled at her and she yelled at me."

Tiggy wanted "a life of her own," but needed a whole new life just to improve her skills with fussy old ladies.

Remember, this is the pre-nicens period.

How do you get a life of your own? She says the idea is ridiculous, especially if you have children, as Tiggy did.

"What life of your own? Your own comfort, space, belongings, home, thoughts?"

Who has their own thoughts? Aren't what pass for "thoughts" the milky residue of media, boiled down to the denominator?

"How are you to have your own life without your own thoughts?

How are you going to get your own thoughts unless you think for yourself?

How can you think for yourself if you don't know what the thoughts were before yours?

"But that would require study! So does having your own life."

Life is make-believe for poor Tiggy

You don't ever get to have a life of your own unless you earn it.

She worked at Strawbridge's in 1930 at $18 a week, (Tiggy is in at $12 an hour), first in fabrics, then in the toy department where the nasty Scotsman gave you a pasty reproof if he found you lounging at end of the day. You got a lunch hour, no breaks, but you could go to the bathroom.

"That was the only place you could sit down."

Well, "that wasn't a life either but nobody said a word 'cause they needed a job." Forty years and a million bucks.

Along the way her new vision makes a mess. She says of the radio in the kitchen: "isn't that awful it's so dirty."

Don't look up at the ceiling. It's hanging down in places.

Anybody can visit old ladies.

Works Cited

Maimonides. **Guide of the Perplexed.** Translated by M. Friedlander. NY: Hebrew Publishing Co. 1881.

Farewell Sorrow

If you want to know about life you want to know about death but nobody will tell you. That's because nobody knows. Talk about romance and tall tales. Nobody knows about death. The proof is everybody lives as if there were no death even at the brink. If you go in for near death experiences of the invisible worlds, good for you. Dairy queen is ice cream in the same way as the process of death in the Tibetan bardo. It's not ice cream at all so let's pretend. Even my wife who has attended countless deaths, signed certificates, held hands, humming, crooning the same songs I hear her sing to infants will only say, nothing but love. If there's one person you would want at your taking off, at the letting go it's her, that's unless you know and love the King of Kings and Lord of Lords, and He's coming to get you, since He knew you before and has walked you this way where He says, because he loves me I will rescue him.

End of an Era

Without knowing in advance, August 25, 2004 is the last time I speak to her in her home. Now she's in the pen.

We need repetitions to get the shifts in life. Right after Carl Bowers had celebrated mass and one hour before he died of a stroke, I put my arms around him and called him Papa, with no self consciousness whatever. In a man's last days a stillness comes. Dean Henry Burlage's stillness made me say that, content with the piles of horse and elephant manure I'd brought him, sitting on the ground in his garden, legs askew around his pale green miniature roses I felt his immense oneness with the moment and the place. Two nights later he took his third and last trip to ER.

Carroll Abbott began to take his leave in dreams, wan and riven with cancer, joking about the Texas Madrone, inspiring me to write a series of facetious takes on native plants, two of which he published at the end. My own grandmother Anna Mack said both hello and goodbye to me in a dream in which I knew more of her in one instant, fifteen years after she died, than I ever knew in life, appearing in the midst of a difficult trial and made her love so clear, saying that I had been given all the gifts.

Another prediction of passing, a longer one of boredom is going to be hers. Bill Holt, weeks prior to his falling from the construction site of an A/C job for the city of Phoenix seemed aggressively abstracted. Not the real case at all, but distracted, a precursor of his taking. In the ICU at St. Joe's, his body swollen double from the fall, packed in ice, his funeral, his widow, the lawsuit, the schemes by the church to take her settlement, all proved otherwise. I feel a like exhaustion in these last calls to her, like her anger in our last visit, a being that despises speech. I see my extensive doodling from the beginnings of this tension on the would be notes for August, '04.

What did we say that last time? That Uncle Paul is an incredible story, 13 stents and then a new transplanted heart! That Bruce will be 56 tomorrow, but the swelling in his brain is coming back affecting his speech and memory. He had another MRI last Thursday, has been on steroids to shrink the fluids, 4 doses a day. More brain surgery at Temple is contemplated by Dr. Laskey who removed the 1st tumor. That a friend of hers, Norm Kelley has esophagus cancer too, with an ultimate faith in the will of God and a faith that he's to be healed. He has a portal in his left shoulder for medication and a machine to dispense meds, takes radiation 5 days a week.

"Every person is different," she says, "body and mind."

A mouse gene, I say, the fast twitch muscle, injected into athletes, triples reaction times.

The original Olympics was blood thirsty she says (she was there).

I tell her I want to raise pet ravens.

She says, we accuse others of our own sins.

She remembers again her brother's tricks with orange drink spiked with alcohol. The men went into the kitchen to get it. "I drank it fast, I was thirsty. I was sweating. I had some more. But no effects."

"Too much of anything and my body protests to my mind." That's what Michelangelo says, but she means DaVinci.

She says that Aeyrie is capable of two careers.

"Tell him Aunt Libby said so," she says.

Hang in there. But do it elegantly.

And then finally comes this. I don't write it down, but how can I forget it?

"I'm not going to commit suicide. I will not consciously do it." Consciousness has along been our resident joke.

Again I fail in recognition, but what comes makes me know it.

9/14/04

On September 14 I call her, Monday, get no answer, but later learn she had checked into the hospital the previous Thursday, as she had planned, to get her gall bladder removed, swearing silence. But not mentioning it, not to tell, cannot say. It's a replay in other terms of whether or not her watercolors existed, to be her theme from now on: "Don't call me. I won't call you. Don't visit either. At least until my lawyer says you can (presumably three days after death). She had announced years before that "it is all taken care of," meaning funeral arrangements, burial, banquet and wake. I kid you not, I skipped them.

When I called Monday and got no answer I thought, maybe she's shopping. So I decided to call the next day. We had just returned from camping for three days on East Baldy above 9000 ft in the mist and rain, reviving our heaven sent 15 year old black chow, somebody she can understand, her own age.

9/15/04

The next day, Tuesday the 15th I call in the morning. There is no answer. I call in the mid afternoon. There is no answer.

I had kept the number from Riddle Memorial Hospital after her hip replacement. I call Mr. Riddle.

Bingo.

Operator transfers to ICU.

ICU tells me they are expecting her from surgery within the hour.

What surgery?

They don't know and swear not to tell if they do. Do I have clearance? She swore not to tell and swore them not to. I call again in an hour, get the same routine about releases, privacy.

All the extremes of contradiction and uncertainty, are compounded by earlier occasions. Like the time my toddler son drank mineral spirits and we got the paramedic ride, but no treatment and took a cab to another hospital. Or the time the Clayton Foundation had me emptying radioactive xylene down the lab drain and cleaning the bottles to save pennies so I could have a liver bilirubin test. I call the hospital the asphodel institution.

My wife's emergencies complicate the affair in my mind, all the way back to her first year internship when she came home in tears when one of her first patients died. The chief intern there was very positive with the patient, but when he exited the room confided to her, "she's dog meat." The dog meat spills over in multiple ER rotations, desperate knife wounds in Dallas, 48 hours on continuous surgical shifts and onto multiple resuscitations in private practice, comatose children carried by their parents into her office wrapped in oregano, declared brain dead by ER docs, but coming back to life. Coming back to life.

The professions are worried for their defense mechanisms. The privacy laws make me feel about the same as I did that Saturday night I was arrested by the Blanco Texas police for driving with a Pennsylvania driver's license. You had to be there to appreciate it. They held me for 4 hours in case I would incriminate myself. Near midnight I was about to entertain the department with verse when they let me go.

I call Bruce, Marvin's son who has made himself a part of her life. Get him at home. Yes he says, she was admitted the previous Thursday, the 9th for an obstruction in the gall bladder. She had turned all yellow, he said. Yes he had been to see her every day, but she told him not to visit today or tomorrow. Gathering my medical resources, I wonder if the surgery was laparoscopic, whether she has pancreatitis too since she was admitted 5 days prior to surgery, a more serious event. Gallstones accumulate from bile salts used to digest fats. Sausages, scrapple?

9/21/04

I provoke other busy bodies into calling. They penetrate the sanctum, learn that she had a tumor under the gall bladder that was malignant.

9/22/04

Because there is no phone in ICU, and she's there a week, it is more then a week before she has a regular room. From my first calls I infer that it is better for females to call female nurses anyway.

This time they are warmer, it must be a new outreach ministry. I hear them humming something in the background, sounds like "The Walls of Jericho."

"Hello."

A little nasal and far away, she says this is the first day she is stable, meaning I suppose anything from that the deluge of visitors has decreased to the opposite.

"Hello. This is your cousin."

"I thought it was my nephew."

"I feel like your grandfather."

She is on clear liquids and the house diet. Soon to be moved to skilled nursing. Has had physical therapy on the 2nd day, but is bored. All the waiting around creates tension. Says she forcefully refused her medication last night, frightened herself and the staff. Has had horrible diarrhea for three days. Can critique the menu. Chicken and rice soup for lunch. Too much meat. Cottage cheese and fresh fruit, too large a serving.

Oncology has been introduced. She says she will take it a day at a time. We don't discuss the medical aspects. I tell I have been informed. They pulled out the catheter this AM.

I tell her that Joggy, who can't see out of one eye, has diminished hearing, very bad hip so he walks like a C, but would anyway walk down any mountain road to its end, is back from the mountain vastly improved.

9/27/04

I call on her last bite of lunch at the Nursing Skills center, Monday after a big
weekend. She sounds placid, says she's just sitting there waiting, is anxious but that it's her head talking, her body has been through it before she says, doing the simpler things. Get up on her feet, ½ lap in the ward, foot, leg exercises, horizontal bars, then lunch. Really she's feeling good which she proves. "Life never turns out the way you think or would hope." Bad habits are better gone, yes and no. Realism.

I never asked her what she had expected. I think it was to live.

The activities director had brought a jumbo cross word book. She, who did the NY Times puzzle for years, threatens to do the whole book in an afternoon, which is like the watercolor session she had at the hip therapy barn. Never told them she was a watercolorist. They asked to hang it. Never told anybody anything.

The Women's church pastor brings Hudson Taylor's biography, first missionary to China, a man of huge fortitude and grace who felt it a necessity to live like the Chinese. Her eyes get tired she says. One of her sister's docs told her back then that when the patient feels better she is better. She is cross-referencing, remembering, probing.

She got a call from nephew Robert in Hawaii. She feels strong. Slams the phone down after 5 minutes. A favorite visiting pastor has entered the room.

"I think we've talked enough."

But Bruce is also admitted to Riddle ICU, has lost the power of speech.

9/29/04

Call every other day, share intelligence, penetrate the mask, what the oncologist said, Datta. Dayadhvam. Damyata. A malignant pancreas has spread to the liver. She took out Friends Life Care years before, when she and Marvin saw the need, so they could remain at home, now she spurns it because the terms are that somebody has to live with her, which she cannot abide.

She has never allowed anyone to stay in her home aside from Aeyrie one night when he was 9, after much cajoling. She won't go back to the house because she doesn't want a roommate. Her plan is to promote her lawyer factotum to executive VP of her life from here on, have him negotiate her entrance into somebody's medical facility, "I have plenty of money." The oncologist has given her an 8% chance at chemo. She declines.

9/30/04

We have a call in to her Doc, hope to hear by noon. Then I will call. I like to be in the know, but won't tell her anything.

It seems only fair.

We won't talk about how she chose Friend's Life Care so she could stay in her home, but she won't, won't, won't have anybody live with her, a condition of that contract. Peace of mind for the elderly is like a harvest where they are shorn by farmers of their homes, etc. Hospice takes a different approach, has not been mentioned, but will be later. Independence run amok.

Is this good news on the day when Vioxx was first banned?

Yesterday 18 red, pink and variegated white rose buds were delivered by courier to our office, but the benefactor was anonymous, not even a card. I have figured it out. It is from a new patient whose father is in much the same, but worse position with whom we have intervened.

I call, 3 PM her time, but company has just finished a visit (I have learned not to mention their names lest they become querulous) and she sounds worn. Where else can you go but to hospital where everyone drops in on you unannounced. You're vulnerable anyway, being grasped by seekers for vital signs, doctors explaining your latest difficulty to teaching teams.

But oncologists are loners, don't travel in packs, so keep up the suspense to hear what new wrinkle might be put. You are surrounded by strangers, maybe in the next bed and their oncologists too or whatever. Your Senior Pastor will get down for the event and come in. Your family Doc will mellow you with the happiness that you can eat and enjoy your food. In this pyrrhic quality of life you can say you are "very satisfied with the physical, psychological and spiritual care." That's actually good.

The church people think you are an angel because only around those who really know you do you act like the devil.

Unbelievably, oncologist # 1 tells you "the bad news" and right away everybody knows. Physical therapy calls up and says considering the news it'd be better if you had the day off. Another condensed day of boredom. Why are they always taking vital signs anyway, are they afraid of losing you?

I ask about Bruce and am told he is some better. The speech therapist asked him if he could name a fruit. He says, casaba. Another troublemaker.

She won't allow any of her "family" to visit. The dying are goal directed. What doesn't contribute to the experience is not tolerated. That is, all of the above, none of the below.

What I said in answer to her question, do you have any questions, was to say I'd been thinking of what happens when somebody takes a trip. The one who leaves is full of expectation. They have their itinerary. The ones who stay are just the opposite. They aren't going anywhere. Not a good argument for staying.

10/6/04

We finally talked to the family Doc. The incidental finding of liver cancer
was unrelated to the gall stones that necessitated the cancer's discovery, otherwise it would not have been discovered. But the liver's function has returned to normal and while it is spotted with small tumors the liver has a huge reserve capacity. She is a little weak from the operation, she gets physical therapy and eats well, gets reactions from the meds maybe, but denies she takes any, calls them "vitamins." I don't know if she's gotten it yet, but events have put her in the position to have a conscious death.

She has schemes for her aftercare but none realized. Her roommate's husband had the nerve to tell her to turn off the TV at 9 PM, which she did, but has since "invoked her patient's rights" and had the roommate removed, probably carried out behind the building. Nobody tells her what to do! Credo. She gets dozens of calls, visits from friends, visits from hospital personnel so has rather completely shut down her talk on the phone to 90 seconds. Over the phone lines I hear <u>elk among the aspens</u> (*Frigg*, Fall/Winter 2022).

> The white barks are singing
> all the day long
> And all night gold
> rains down
> Fountains of light
> before dawn.

I'm glad I talked to her when no one else did. For years I was the only diversion of a dark day.

I've been reading over and over this one sentence, "love always protects, always trusts, always hopes, always perseveres." I don't find any room here for what I really feel so I'm glad for previous sentences like, "love is patient, love is kind. It does not envy, it does not boast, it is not proud. It is not rude, it is not self-seeking, it is not easily angered...."

How can you be angry? How can you not be angry?

10/19/04

In the space of weeks she went from home to hospital to skilled nursing to the Monticello House life care of Riddle Village, 515A, assisted living, therapy and dining room for 60 beds, semi-private room, social worker. She is on the list for a private, but there are only two, allocated informally. She wants no company or visits. She doesn't want to put anybody out, impose any of her own problems.

I get very changeable responses. That generation felt like they had been imposed upon. She has been in her new single room about a week, things are settling down. She backs off her prohibitions. Her attorney is to handle "everything," the listing of her house foreseen when the benefits retire. He tells me she wouldn't see Jerry, made him leave his flowers and depart unshriven, but Bruce visits she says, but Bruce is himself under orders of a call. She has call forwarding at home so she still receives greetings from the usual people. She says that she gets Lasix for the swelling in her ankles, hates it, but we do not want to burden others.

She verbalizes an apparent confusion of plans to visit her in these new conditions with a visit to her old house, which is an unconscious concern that she will never go there again, but doesn't really want it all to be pillaged and sacked by estate agents. Instead she says she has told the attorney to leave lots of yellow pads around so people can write down what they take. She doesn't tell the attorney. Everybody is in a separate selected, need to know envelop. Now she thinks there's going to be an exhaustive inventory, but the whole estate, sentimental and antiquarian remains bedside. Clear your visits with the neighbor and the attorney!

It must be hard to grasp what you are saying when you have not been outside in 6 weeks. She had a dizzy spell before dinner today, b/p down. She had just had juice and salad when I called. They are giving her miracle drugs like Zantac for anxiety: "the nurse is aware that I am under pressure from so many directions." She had just taken her second Zantac. I cannot elicit what these pressures are except, she says, Lasix. Lawyer appointment tomorrow? Social Worker visits? Listing the house? Letting go of the house? The collection of buttons? Maybe it's her personal appearance and weakness, still she seems to say that I should come and visit her.

There is talk of bringing her chair from home to her room.

10/20/04

Her attorney actually calls me after meeting with her to the effect that she doesn't want any visitors, to postpone them and that she will tell him when she does.

Her worries, closing a joint account still open with Marvin, loose cash in the house, a contribution in memorial of a friend, a conference with the Home next week when she will apply for a private. Her present roomie watched the Red Sox beat the Yankees last night. She borrows $7 from her father attorney! I infer that this generation's independence is the basis of their love. Once independence is surrendered love is compromised.

10/27/04

The medical opinion is that the patient "shouldn't get too stimulated over the house."

"Don't come too soon." She seems to equate a visit with her house, can't imagine we would come to see her.

I had called her, a week ago or so and she indicated a visit would be welcome. Lawyer calls next day after the meeting with her and says she had told him to declare that when she wants a visit she will tell him. She is following her mother's course in being the last months in a home before death. If she can't have a daughter she'll have no one.

10/28/04

Black Bird Green Light

I get her right after lunch, due for a health conference in 2 hrs with the directors and lawyer, her screenplay is under consideration. It's about whether she gets her private room today, needs a new TV, can get dressed on her own now, except the pressure stockings, walks with a walker; has "pensioned off" the wheelchair, hasn't used it in a week. She confirms the factotum's call telling me when or when not to visit.

She goes to gym in A.M. gets hot packs, has other PT activities, an enlarged social schedule. Many more visits than at home, mega ditto phone calls. Nothing like an institutionalized invalid to bring good Samaritans out. People call about the dead. Pastor Bill for Kathy McDowell, whose funeral was at Lima, for information for the church bulletin. She gets a spin off of 3 visitors from the funeral, Dee and Bud Krasner come. Bruce's mother in law tells Lib on the QT that Bruce is racing downhill slalom to a nursing home.

Who put them both thru college? Grandfather Jacob L. What about the 6 or $7000 he sent Howard?

"Some of that came back to Anna." Who knows how much. Why did neither of them ever credit Jacob for their college education?

"It wasn't just one thing."

I know who the favorite man of your life was. Oh. She's interested.

Your father.

"I think you're right." She recounts his counsel again when the Presbyterian friends found out she wasn't baptized, as foregoing the wage of the Mennonite summer school. I egg her on. She admits, "I could best handle money," like her father. She proves it in the end, Miss Carnegie. How to explain her father's intelligence? I mention love. "He went away to school, to Easton, traveled to NY, had a lot of friends." She hopes his postcards are in a box in the attic, not forever lost, thinks they will add to my picture of him.

I see this Indian lying on stilts, bed elevated from the ground, taking letters and mementos into the afterlife. Why do they wait till they're gone?

I tell her Elizabeth is to become the corporate grammarian for her Insurance Co. in Scotland. She is getting about the business of life. That's a joke.
She takes it seriously.

Ha. I say goodbye. I'm not going to keep you girl, I say.

"Here they call you baby, sweetie, honey pie." There is no end of supply of the southern nanny. Either severe regression to the womb or to neutralize the nasty.

We know about the nasty I tell her.
My wife is a doctor.

"Oh."

Yes the nasties are everywhere but she treats them as if she were a saint. I need to get her a religion where she can be a living saint.

"Do you know of one?"
"Does anybody?"

I ask her again whether she told the factotum to tell me when to visit. After she dies he acts so proprietary I want to ask him if he ever kissed her. But by then I have wearied of the dance.

Green Light

"Well, I'm waiting for the green light," I say, like traffic is stacked up overhead, as if the President has landed. Gridlock on the interstate.

Or are they ravens, relatives taking expensive plane trips for maybe a 2 hour visit?

Who do the mementoes belong to, the living or the dead, I wonder. Later I find out they had belonged to the dead many years. They were just stored in her attic.

I don't tell her how these 3 Cooper's hawks sat on the phone pole across the street yesterday. Who were they calling on one wonders? Isn't it illegal to tap the phone line? A hazard of living in the desert, the big birds come in when the weather gets cool and it rains.

I don't tell her that the day Aeyrie got notice that he'd been selected to enter the Western Eye exhibition, where one of the photographs would be purchased for the permanent exhibition, that that morning, in the slanting sun, a full grown golden eagle landed in the birdbath in my back yard. In my mind it is still there. In my mind she, her mother, sister and brother.

Do these blackbird voices mean anything to the transients? She has a lot of paper near by, pretends she's only just started to take notes. Makes this one.

"Andy, green light."
What on earth will tomorrow bring?

11/2/04

Four days later a message on my machine. Evening.

"This is Aunt Libby. Don't call in more than a half hour."

I am too late. Next morning there are two calls, one message in a faint voice, "you are cleared to call Carol Watkins November 3, 4 or 5 around noon to arrange visit."

I come home after badgering tennis balls with Shakespeare. Told the boys of the conflict of business and art. Who's your favorite poet?

I call her right after lunch, on her new number, her private room.

I have the green light.

"I'm not coming to see your house you know."

"When do you want me to come."

"Not before 10 AM."

She has had to change all the addresses on her magazine subscriptions. It will take her till June she thinks.

No, when in weeks and months?

I ask, "is there something you want me to take from your house? Where are the photographs of your father, the watercolor of Jesse."

"You're welcome to anything in photographs. Marvin's album of old plane stamps is in the cocktail table of living room. Old photographs are in the bottom of the wardrobe in the back bed room. The watercolor is in the little chest in the hall, in blue plastic. You can do pretty much what you want."

What you really want to do is take them to dinner and a show.

11/13/04

I call to confirm a visit. Yesterday she got her easy chair and lamp delivered. Says it's too bad they have to be in a hospital instead of her house. The observation raises questions. She, "if anybody had told me I would have to endure this I couldn't possibly." Articulate, "I am busy making myself happy, being cheerful to people. I got an idea from a meditation book about putting monsters in the closet so that's what I do with the possibilities of what I may have to go through. I put them in the closet." But her monsters turned into such wimps. Terminal, but on aspirin? Does she believe in the favor of God in a quiet death?

11/24/04

Her lawyer cooks his turkey in two parts. First soaked in brine and cooked, then the white meat is removed and the brown meat cooked later while the white is kept moist.

She is now a thoroughly institutionalized turkey so we talk about gassing cats. You see the connection. Somebody we can't mention but who you know has just mercifully gassed their cat. These are quality of life issues? My nephew doesn't have the guts to get rid of his. I ask how she'd like to be done. She says her brother nearly did himself one time gassing cats in the garage with good old carbon monoxide. She says she has no thoughts except that the monster is behaving in his closet. I close with, "Aunt Libby, my friend, my aunt.

She, "my ancestor."

11/30/04

Various birds descend. Susan, Christy, Robert, Cynthia etc. are coming to visit December 16th or so. She says she hopes she won't be too vegetative from the medications when they come. Aspirin can just loop you out. Too vegetative, she has these observations that provoke silence in me. Four or five thoughts come at the same time and none of them permit expression. After all, it's a little late to say what I want after so many years.

She introduces the notion of selecting the day of your death, gives some examples. I tell her, not that I'm in denial, that as far as I'm concerned she's not going to die, not to of course limit her choices in any way, can't have that, but what death? They say the creed all their lives then when it matters they renege? "Life everlasting!" I've known her all my life, but it is inevitable that this attitude will be taken.

She told the factotum that she's heard that Drs. can identify the last two weeks, so she says she'll just give him a call, sort of a snooze alarm, but he didn't like that much, maybe he likes her more than is good for him, as other men have. He'll get over it. She is just not forthcoming to the male race. I have an advantage over them because I knew her before she knew that I knew her. She didn't know I was conscious during all the embraces and hugs and kisses. She didn't know I was conscious as a five year old sleeping in her bed. She says I think she's a saint. But I have to tell her others do, not me. I know her.

She absolutely crowed at her announcement that she was marrying Marvin. Felt like she really put one over that time.

I used to taunt her horribly about the greeting card profanations of Easter and Mother's Day that occasioned Snowden's Department Store. Pro mercantile, she said, don't you believe in Mother's Day? The graphologist was right about her, "while you possess much emotional depth, you do not make it a practice to display your feelings."

Since she's selecting the day of death she has already counseled a Catholic lady on the afterlife from *John* 14, which she now quotes to me and says "you get a new body but it may be spiritual, you will recognize each other, but there will be no gender." The lady says, "say it again, say it again." Since you're going to see people in heaven I ask her, when I die are you going to come running up to me and say na na na na? She's not going to bite on that one either. We bandy Lewis's *Great Divorce* with the grass and light so real they hurt your feet and eyes.

No, she says, she's doing pretty well on her new pain schedule. A Tylenol every four hours and now a small Percocet at night that gives hallucinations from 9:30 to 11:30. Has had a good intellectual talk with Senior Pastor about the end of things.

I tell her that volume 2 of the 3, *A Tulip Blooms from the Heart*, is going to be ready and sent to her in pre-proof next week. How it's all about love. She quotes Thornton Wilder, Bridge of San Luis Rey "…but the bridge is love." Yes it's love, love in love about love in life. Beginning or end, alive or dead, as they said, the old and young remember each other. The young are influenced by the old to a thousand generations of those that love Him. Still going.

Here's their story I tell her, going through the table of contents by memory, you're last sweetheart. Henry is first, tragedy, gravity, humor, laughter, joy. All you Pennsylvania nuts. She's said for years she comes of a line of peasants back to Adam. It's because they ate wheat and the Italians ate pasta, she maintains. Food makes the man. The individual character traits, the strengths are common to the community.

As if I'm getting too close she says she never liked having her picture taken, tells me of the worst picture she ever took was in 1944 when she was a plane spotter. In that day planes were everywhere and people took shifts on the roof of the Media courthouse to forestall the Nazis, sending warning descriptions downtown for analysis. She worked in the Chestnut Street branch, her own version of MI 5. Had to get clearance. One morning they herded them into a prison-like room at 4 AM and took their pictures. Yes she destroyed it, a jail mug.

No, I don't think you're going to die, I say. Henry and Anna and Flo and Howard and Jay and Bea are still living, still challenging youth with their lives' boundaries. I know you sweetheart.

She says people are praying for her.

Can I pray for you.

Yes.

Can I pray for you now.

Yes.

Can I pray for you out loud?

Yes.

I do.
We say goodbye.

12/7/04

Call around 5. No answer. Call again. No answer. Resisting calling Mr. Riddle again, I call again.

So you're still there?

Yes, on the new regime of Tylenol, and wowsie, just had a Percocet.

Are you hallucinating?

No, but she's learning to ask for help. There are these rituals of self defense where she has a box of tissues and flashlight on one side of the pillow, call button on the other, feet slightly exposed at the bottom of the bed. Has hot feet!

We talk of releasing life.

She told factotum: "I had written up an obituary but I guess I lost it. I guess I can do another one for you before you need it."

Mellow.

Says she has told her Pastor she wanted no family eulogies. Said what Robert and I did at the parents' occasion was a sibling contest. I'm silent.

But she wants to fight about it, says, well you're being awfully silent. You think her finger is on the call button here? Is there any shock value in the remark?

She sees the world through ideas and eyes that oppose romance is what I would say if I replied. I tell her that I'm practicing negative capability, holding in mind two conflicting truths without having to choose between them [Keats]. Just sittin' releasing.

I ask why her sister claimed she was the family deviant. She says she always thought Flo had an abnormal immune system because she got twice what others got only once, that she even contracted impetigo from one of her students in her first teaching job. As to the sister's religion, who was only 10 when her father died, uncle Will, having a daughter her age, Gladys, sent both to camp with the Reformed. Later Flo was Presbyterianized.

Lib says she has warned Pastor that family is going to descend on her death. So he should look out. But I'm descending now, it's Thanksgiving, seat belt fastened. She saw her picture in *A Tulip Blooms from the Heart*, says it was taken at 15 ½ for her school year book, that Jake's letters were really pathetic in their presenting the view that he was caring for his grandchildren. Grind his bones.

Her façade is opaque, referring to her letters therein. Somehow she thinks I have earlier letters. I don't. She says she had mixed feelings at her father's death. That Anna tried to give her children normalcy in that June of '29, after Grandfather Jake's death, had a house party at graduation at Penn State where she was a house mother, then a surprise birthday party for Lib's 19th. Sounds rather a celebration.

She is pleasantly surprised that Carole Watkins stayed up all night reading her book, A Red Portfolio. I tell her it needs to be called Conversations with a …. We can add different words here depending. She says that although Bea was always kind to Rena she also always thought her an intruder and never warmed to her. And who has Lib ever warmed to? I told her that when grandfather Edwin Arthur Yeo and Rena visited in Pittsburgh I had heard my mother say words to this effect and as soon as they arrived went up to Rena and told her "I think you're pretty." As to saving Browns Mills from the auction block she quotes Shakespeare "be not the first by which the new is tried…." Meaning, bear realistically the fact that loss wins. Unfortunately for my decreasing sympathy for realists I think loss sucks. *Cast a cold eye on death. Horseman pass by.*

Keep a low key. Even keel. Don't keel over, is that it? Don't rock the baby. Releasing life.

I should send her *Chang Pomes*. Then she would complain I've gone from garrulity to brevity.

On the theology of sin and self examination she says she can't help, i.e., after charging sibling rivalry at two funerals, she missed her biweekly shower attending a jazz *Te Deum* concert at the Rest Home, strings, oboe, viola, violin, everything but a harp. That's coming. Saints or sinners, I can't make up my mind. Joey & Melissa, Robert, Cynthia, Sue, Christy, Nick, then, as of 12/26 Aeyrie , me, Anne.

I say, do you remember who I am.

She says "I can't forget it."

Always opaque, she says "we feel we have to protect the image we have of ourselves, therefore we say nothing or everything." She calls that learning to ask for help. Still interested in dying on demand, the old folks grapevine has it that within certain limits people can die when they want to, that is after they have accomplished their desires. The aged are culpable of myth and fantasy, scheme with cunning. The underbelly of the institution, the secret code of the resigned, spreads in little cocktail hours and wine tastings mostly, always among the little old ladies, who glow and giggle to each other about how they want to die. And here's where they share the initiated secrets. They tell each other how. Then they boast to their sons and daughters, like they just got an A on their assignment, that they know how to do it.

In some sense if our senses are tuned, she is more beautiful than she has ever been, the pink chair she sits in, reupholstered, has silver thread silk and rose. Sometimes she wears a pink sweater. The appearance is delighting. The white hair flies over the sides of her head.

She jokes that the hair makes them think she's an angel. It's a little spare, flying just the same, a halo around the sun on fall days in the mountains when the aurora whitens. The brow, since we are in the mountains now, is a cliff with patches whitened in the blizzard. Looking at the landscape, a little *locus amoenus,* you know, the lovely place of Virgil is not the nature of the golden age, but the silver verge of afterlife, beauty swallowed up in light, because beauty is the highest flesh can come to it. Virgil, before the Renaissance, had "the ram himself in his pasture to change his fleece's color." (5) See the gold flower in her face? *They believe a certain godly nature to be in the gold.* Black wires turn to white, the silver wings, the mild accepting eye.

Sure there are other ways to go, in a flash of youthful exuberance not gentle, all fleshed up, but consider the true case, the case of the vine raising its "clusters on the neglected thorn" (*Fourth Eclogue,* 5). These human garden spots like grass, a residue greater than memory of spiritual fruit of the life they don't see or we either in a suspended natural law, the corn gold, the ox with the lion, earth recreated. Where silver is can gold be far behind? In the midst of Broadway this is exaggeration? The Lord himself shall descend from heaven with a shout.

If hallowed means softened, she had not lost her temper until some days after the Thanksgiving visit, then signs off the phone with a bite. Do you want beauty in the flesh, the dreaded subcutaneous layers shimmering slightly, intact in the walk? Or with the deeper being, the one you love to life around, the faithful kind, your own mother if you like, when the years of gravity have peeled the face, bone, brow, the jaw await resurrection?

On the verge she won't play my game any more than I play hers. She wants to say something outrageous to provoke me. I want her to speculate, something she disdains as purely a male phenomenon, a thing beneath her.

"When you come running up to me when I get to heaven what are you going to say?"

She really wants to tell me is that she has found another misspelled word or a factual error in this manuscript.

12/9/04

It is December 9. I planted a red oak last year. Its leaves now are changing shades of red, vermillion, scarlet, maroon to end in brown. Across the street a cottonwood turns gold. Leaves shower the street, covered in gold. I pull back the curtain, sit in a chair and watch. Maturity is not a new thing. Get it? Just disrespected among youth who have such grave reserve of authority.

Not to offend, it suggests her relatives should get in touch with their eternal selves. Look at the last name on the driver's license. Equivocating Everyman, something I've always wanted to do, it's just as old world as ever. It isn't a new world anyway.

Sadly for puerility, the last name combines meanings of both completion and maturity. It is Tolkien's ring and winter's age, white hoarfrost, the man-woman ripe, fulfilled like the lieder in the northern ear. They snipped off their braids of hair and stored them in the trunks. Now I've got them.

Effort satisfied doesn't suggest death as much as progeny and ancestry. The bone-hard skeleton of principle, virtue proven circumstances, a solo 90 year old who converses first with God each day. Who wants to grow old? Everybody. Maturity balances, reconciles, adjusts. Youth exaggerates, advocates, accelerates. Less is more, we say. Arrested development is not maturity. Ironically, maturity prolongs youthfulness, decreases lines, diminishes toil, fret and care. "Well, you have to learn it for yourself." (Ecclesiastes 8:1).

12/15/04

She can't understand how all the obese women on her floor maintain their weight with the rations. She worries for their handlers' effort in moving all that mass. This is in the middle of last family visits. Joe III and Melissa last weekend, Robert, Susan, this. They have not called to confirm. Don't expect it. I tell her it could get better, communication, because when people get older they get wiser? She says that visiting a relative on the way out reminds them of family. She is being nice.

I amuse her with my vigilance and care of my children, because she sees that some people at 60 divest themselves of children. Maybe they don't realize how long it takes to grow up, 38 years. Depending on their choices that is nearer or farther. Look at Milton. The modern shudders. Milton was close to and dependant on his father until this age. You don't want your children to grow up to be Milton do you?

She says she expects it of me, look at my care at extending the life of our old dog. Other people would have gassed him she says, because he is an analogical joke between us. "You won't get rid of him as long as I'm alive." Sadly this is not true. He left us Palm Sunday, she waited till the Saturday after Easter. He's blind in one eye, can't hear, his right hip makes him walk in a circle sometimes, he's incontinent at best. Can't get up and can't sit down, has to have 5 minute breaks when he walks across the street, pants like he's run a mile. His last days were heart breaking.

I don't tell her that Joggy has been an agent of God in deliverance to our family. God can work in a dog. Sounds like a story from *Guideposts*. He can't really stand up unless he leans against something. When he leans on me it is just about as precious as rocking your son to sleep at 3 AM when he has a fever. He perks up when he sees another dog just about the way she does when visited. Makes her feel a little special for people to fly out to see her from the ends of the earth. But you don't have to worry, earth isn't going to end, death is going to be swallowed up in victory.

She says she's still not in total agreement about my effort to collect and distribute her things. I tell her, just say so and I'll cancel it. But she says, oh no. Far be it from her to make decisions. One of my tennis buddies is going to give away his wife's wedding ring! Well why not. The people in the Nest church gave theirs in the offering plate, along with their 54 Chevy Belair. Another guy gave the royalties for his talking book, $110,000. Just stood up and announced it. I myself bought a huge share in the restoration of the Christian Reformed grammar school. In a way I considered it reparation for Jacob. Christians giving away, one time we took 11 large boxes of medical supplies and drugs to St. Vincent De Paul. Just carried it up to their storeroom. Sent also a large amount to missionaries in Thailand. In those days if you were in leadership in any way at all you got invited to a dinner in the Nest sanctuary and afterward pledges and checks were taken.

The first time you think it is maybe a dinner of appreciation.

Furniture is auctioned off. My grandfather's tables and chairs and copper kettles. His letters gone. This old world.

Farewell sorrow,
praise God the open door,
I ain't got no home in this world anymore.

Her original opinion was that hers was all tawdry used junk anyway. So what do you care what happens to it? Do you reject the body, the material? Spurn the flesh? Immolate temptation? Up in smoke. Are you only your physical body? Is that a heresy, the rejection of the body, or shall we keep it under. Mind/body opposition. Marriage is honorable in all? Do you know what happens in marriage people? Like she says, in heaven there is no gender. Get it while it's hot. The earth is the Lord's, he has given us the dominion of his hands. Make up your mind.

Opposition or union. Earth or heaven. Sow to the flesh, reap the spirit? "I believe in the "communion of the saints, the forgiveness of sins, the resurrection of the body, and life everlasting." They all think they're going to live eternally in heaven, but that's the joke, they won't be there even five heavenly minutes when oops, it's back down to earth again. Then the passenger pigeon and the buffalo, the Apache but not the businessman will thrive. The prairie restored. The oceans pure. Do you have a vision of the afterlife? The new heavens and the new earth. Read to the end. Do you hear the Mennonite here? Put not your trust in horses.

Her visitors are praising my art on her wall and the *Tulip* on her table. Her lawyer wants to take Aeyrie's 16x20 print home when she dies, which she is thinking about doing while they are considering history. The earth wave on the wall changes colors in the light and gets comments. Now she calls me Bozzy, a humor invoking James Boswell, Dr. Johnson's biographer. I think I am learning to write. She says nobody has ever been able to understand what I wrote. Reductionists. Realists. Let us not prize ordinary men.

Visitors want to borrow the *Tulip*. It helps to be told by the press that beauty and truth are some kind of democratic thing, It depends on the press. The puzzle has many pieces and the more you fill in the better *Tulip* and *Portrait* show the huge conflict between my childhood memories and the present person she is, the great unexplained silence of conspiracy about Mennonites.

Odd notes left over. The house next door, 198K. If she sells for that she can live on it a year and a half at $300 a day plus lawyer's fees. There's only one electric line to the attic. That explains it! Jerry broke the plumbing, cost her $67. She also thinks I'm Bozzy because Boswell rewrote. Her friend Betty wants to write. The watercolor yellow forsythia in the turquoise vase was kept by the school.

Don't Drive At Night

This chronology is failing. In between and among I fly Christmas night to Philadelphia and drive a truck the 3000 miles to LA with all that entails. New Year's eve in Arkadelphia, Aeyrie's favorite. He is another driver. I end up with all the papers worth mentioning, things never known that need to be identified. There are calls, but they partake of tensions aroused by the move. I'm talking on the phone with her, somehow about pain. She covers hers, goes on offense, had been saying that you can't call cancer arthritis. I tell her, attempting sympathy, that serious pain of the body I find difficult. She laughs, mocks again that when she and her sister, maiden aunts, visited me in the hospital after the medial cartilage was removed from my knee they had a good laugh at my "pain." Risk-taking laughter. There were three of them if you count their mother. They only tolerated the one son and brother.

I'm irritated with her realism, celebrating her own pain with self glorifying stoicism. Boasting you have cancer. Zero *gelassenheit.* She wanted to go on sorting clothes on top of the dryer, pretending to be a non-thinking circle member, still afflicting the Acme, yakking on the phone about nothing. The amazing thing I have realized just this morning is that she didn't want to die any more than my black chow.

Two similar cases of insurmountable will, but it is really spirit do you know. For six months I expected that dog to be gone by morning, but then there he would be, hungry and ready to walk, if you could call it that. One time I had to carry him home in my arms. I noticed then how light he had become. Even his last week he could jog to the gate if there were another dog passing, then he would collapse out of breath. One time he had a severe fit from the noise of the lawn mower, but he even came back from that.

The night before he died he lay on the bed we had made, panting with the will to life, a heating pad beneath his body, and about 10 PM began to bark as he always had when he knew his family was coming home. He would bark in anticipation for several minutes before his mistress' car ever came into sight. How did he know? It was his welcome bark, deep and commanding. He barked for life all those night hours. We put our hands on him and he stopped and heaved for breath. Then he barked. He barked hour after hour and only then did it begin to get fainter. It was Palm Sunday.

I stayed home while the others went to church. But I didn't know what to do. I think maybe I expected him to get up and run. But he stayed panting. His mistress came back in an hour. She has shepherded plenty of souls to the door of the afterlife, held their hands when they were alone, sung to them, somehow communicating the comfort. She sat with him, her hands on his chest and brow. I came out to check. He breathed his last. Then we wept. There was never any of the spirit of resignation in him, as sick as he was, never any give.

I heard accounts of Anna Elizabeth's passing. Betty Miller held her hand, sat with her for hours. So did Carole Watkins, others. Just 5 days before, she was angry that she had had an electrical short in the brain, was partly paralyzed, had to be fed. She died in her sleep though, but in Ira Byock's *The Four Things That Matter Most* list, please forgive me, I forgive you, thank you and I love you, she only said the last. That's what she meant when she said she didn't think things would turn out as they did. She did not expect to die.

I had wanted to catalogue her affairs in a manner of speaking, but was confronted with relatives' doubts and hers. Family doubters said, better do nothing, what will come of something? Anything to prevent the salvation of the body. They want to save their own points of view. You can't drive all that way. One, how can you do it? Two, the weather will prevent it. Three, she doesn't want it done. Their doubt made me doubt them. The people on the sidelines are nuts.

Curator of the family. She says that's what I had called her years ago. Every family needs one if they are to be a family in any larger sense. After looking into the Macks these few years she never thought to mention that Lizzie and Jesse had their pictures in the old photo album in the attic. This after countless queries about old photographs.

Now that those letters exist in printed form in *Tulip* it seems as though they have always been, but of course that isn't so. The pieces of the puzzle change in the light like the painting on her wall, like the desire to understand. What is permanent ? When Grandfather Henry Mack was 90 I was 5. Don't sell the little children short, "a little child shall lead them." I entertained the new Jacob, he's two. He took home a stuffed white kitty cat bigger than himself. Remember me! She's getting communion at 11 AM today.

If glory is going to be revealed in us, in families, in the earth, it is to be in our deeds and the attitudes of our hearts. The hymn of the realist is sung by the Preacher. "I the teacher." And what does he teach, "what is twisted cannot be straightened; what is lacking cannot be counted." By this measure we are done for. No healings or miracles today. No surmounting all odds. The realist opposes faith, but faith is all that matters. The statement "I am dying of cancer" is the realist's credo. Realism is a death sentence. The easy road. "You can't come back from a deficit. That's just realism." When you're dead you're dead. Realism and ignorance opposite the heroic.

The way I believe it, God resolves opposites, reverses natural expectation. The big problem is the preacher's natural mind. If the Virgin Mary had told her Mom that she was pregnant her Mom would have said, "it takes two honey." Natural expectation covers every degree of "normal" expectation. Thus, the way things are, the sick must die, the rejected fail. But revelation contradicts every natural state, turns rough places plain, virgins conceive.

Passing revelation through the natural understanding confirms all opposites. Passing the natural through revelation reverses them, brings union, deliverance. Thus religion is bondage. Everybody can cite abuses and failure of revelation, but never of natural expectation because the natural never fails. You don't need faith just a little bit of doubt.

Revelation is the pretext to reconciliation among ourselves, turning offense to blessing. You can explain this process to the natural mind endlessly. The natural mind transfers its assumptions to all it perceives. People do this too. They transfer all they assume to be true about light, space, science to anything that conflicts with it and believe it wrong. Even if they haven't finished high school they have dogma. There is a dog in dogma. The issue isn't, do I agree with revelation, but do I like the salvation of God and as they say in Hebrew, the name of salvation in Yahshua.

Everything can be restored. What's the point of holding a grudge in the afterlife if you can't get satisfaction. What's the point of keeping a scorecard for real and imagined losses and transgressions in this life that reach far into the past if you can't even the score.

But there doesn't need to be a purpose for the techniques of human self destruction. We can resurrect the offenders and torture them in a Dantean fugue, rehabilitate them in the halfway house. Sounds good. Or stand up to them while they're in the flesh. So stand up! They wanted money from Jake, so when he offended them they didn't oppose him. They went begging, swallowed their pride and it stuck in their craw. Weakness created resentment. Saving the appearances to their own benefit. His grandson stood up to Jake and then extorted him. How does that make you feel, brother, compromised?

Here's the problem with the Way of Jesus. After you've made your best case, rehearsed it again and again, brooded over it, cursed the deed and darkness, he tells you, bless those who curse you, bless and curse not. Pray for them that persecute you. This probably doesn't mean break their teeth. It probably means to loose love and peace upon them, blessing. Ouch, the cup of water is the liquid presence of the Comforter. So what do you do with the offenders?

By the time you grow up and age out old dogs can tell you, and my neighbor across the street, a curmudgeon who worked for the Indian bureau, had stacks of Playboy to the wainscot, took care of everybody's business, he got old. It was a slalom bounce from car to post to house, landing akimbo to cross the street. Wherever his mind wanted to go, he sent his body.

But my dog is worse, he can't see, hear, or walk, but he can eat. Put him out of his misery, put him down, put the body down they all say. But his mind is as alive as ever. Just like the Dutch torturers in the *Martyr's Book* thought they could kill the Anabaptist body and the mind would die. That's backwards. You can't kill the mind, it lives, communicates its passions when the body is gone. Even the memory of neighbor Hank and his desert tortoises has meaning, drew youths to own his house that are every bit as wacko as he. They stand in the street and stare at cars going 30.

By this standard nothing can be lost, even when it is unmade it will out, someday be remade. How do you want it, via Jung's collective Orange County, an OC where cousin Geoffrey is a watercolorist, or in the eternal library where all the lost works of merit and all works done by people of merit exist? They more than exist, they're eternal. You heard about this? Want to get on Google and find it? It's not in the Alexandrian Library either. It's a little like the last work of Traherene, *Poems of Felicity*, manuscripts found in the British Museum accidentally, published in 1910, 200 years after his death, or Tolkien's essay on Beowulf of 1936 published in 2003 in its unrevised form, about 400 pages. There are reputations waiting to be made or lost in the afterlife. Consider if that one copy of *Jerusalem* had been lost.

Families have made comebacks too when they were reduced to one. J. Howard was the only son of the only son, keep that up long enough and it leads to extinction. But what about them that never were but were supposed to be, that got aborted, the lost coin, pearl, orphan? I guess we call these promises. The world where the lion lies down with the lamb revives the fetuses, the progeny of childless Abraham as the sands of the sea. Is that the difference between the works of man and the works of God? The first is possible the second is certain, that is, after the fact. Post cognito! But if they are works of man they can be done by men. If a man made it a man can fix it. Are we just referring here to frakturs, diaries, records, letters? Once lost they can be found, if they exist, but if they have ceased to exist? Maybe in our time or not, the resurrection. The resurrection of the body leads to the heavenly record. Do you mean the Father has kept all those letters?

Yes.

That's why they call it redemption. It brings back what is lost. All these Anabaptists believe it, that in rejecting the body, the book, the oeuvre, they actually help it along, like living in sin that grace may abound? Such a lot of questions just to understand that nothing is lost. Say it together now, nothing is lost. I know my redeemer lives. After the restoration when the mammoth lies down under the terebinth you will wish you had known that it would be so wonderful, because at the time it would have helped. What does Isaiah say, "Lord open his eyes that he may see." Nothing is lost. Saved to the uttermost. Only regrets are lost. Not one species, not one baby, not one attempt to put into the body, into form what all creation groans toward, the redemption of the body.

Not only are the lost ones to be restored to a magnitude above all expectation but you've also got to get over this notion of physical existence as a curse. It has been turned to a blessing by Jesus.

4/6/05

She calls me this AM, 4/6 four days after her death with the info that she has a "Washington Jefferson," 1766, one of twenty. She is back in her house, looks a little younger and pulls the b/w print carefully from its envelop, the tissue paper slides off. Do you like the symbolism? She says she was never able to get a price on it. Yes it is a dream. And I had another last night. Her skin is fair, she is in her kitchen, about forty years old. My dog is hanging out too, head down, humpbacked, like in his last months, curled head to tail. But there are dreams and then there are visions. In the vision I had of him Easter Sunday at communion that dog was running flat out in those tight circles that he loved, barking and barking and barking, carousing around the throne of God.

Afterlife isn't necessarily life eternal, especially when it comprises your attorney's behests, set in motion before, but carried out now, even if some of them are made gratuitous, like a black windowed limo taking 6 people across town for a half hour to a grave and then bringing them back to the memorial and lunch. Anything after death is after life so yes the dead do speak, their factotums want to know what size black limo, their bereaved want to know how big a basket of flowers. Since the coffin is closed it makes you wonder who after all is checking on these things. Sure the attorney needs the SS #, but he is only liquidating the estate not the family. Attorneys don't judge so the fact you're not going to be there, is, well, understood.

My dead bodies shall revive. You will not suffer your holy one to see corruption.

4/20/ 2005

There are some notes on pieces of paper left over from the end of the process. Her house in order to be sold had to be cleaned, etc. There was difficulty with the use and occupancy permits, termites, plumbing waste pipes cracked, the kitchen floor taken up. So the house as a metaphor of the self was renovated. Repaired, renewed. She told me that in her dreams she used neither walker nor cane. Nor in her mind. Of her surviving beyond expectation she says that "they look at me suspiciously." We know who they are, the functionaries of death, aids, clerks, pastors, friends, relatives.

Waking dreams fantasizing: selective memory. Bechtels. Cousin Jesse in the lap of Aunt Florence. A separate snapshot.

Anna's first language was English at home. Of the Berks Co. bureau, Annie had that from before, left to her by her grandmother.

One week before she died she was angry because she couldn't move her right hand from a TIA. Later paralysis spread to her arm and she had to be fed, but only for less than a week.

Rimbaud's Attic

There's a lot of nonsense written about Rimbaud. That he was an angel, fallen or otherwise. That he had a destiny other than his own. Nobody has a destiny until after the fact of earning it. Not that he hyped himself for the ages to be greater than he was, lived a grand lie in competition with all the other great liars of politics and literature. Let him rest in the grave, even if in going there he contradicted all that the free thinkers and licensees want, because in his end all he wants is peace with God. What else is there anyway?

Rimbaud has been called a saint for struggling with his own savage nature. Up close the savage nature is heightened in the old survivor, they are not at all what you first thought or lived with all of life. That Rimbaud walked out on the false world of culture and civilization, that he denuded his spirit of artificial trappings or wanted to doesn't sound all that bad. That was his notion of Christmas on earth.

Well in the interim there is fame, achievement, fortune. Are these what is destined and is destiny greater than honesty? She doesn't answer any of this, turns her back on the lesser by default and chooses the greater, is that her thinking? A better question might be, does it matter at all?

Put fame and fortune in a scale and weigh it against self sacrifice, honesty and the life of the mind to no end other than itself. The mind as an end in itself, what a notion. And add that no one would know of it. There's your Rimbaud. None of these delights shared with the world. Is it a crime, a shame, a sin, a loss?

You have to answer it yourself, unless you see fame as arbitrary, and an obstacle to truth's realization and beauty's. Does it matter at all? Is not the thing an end in itself and not the means to some other end? Can't anybody shut Socrates up? Is beauty beauty if it is a means to fame? Vice versa. That could be an implicit argument of her life. That it doesn't matter. What matters is truth, honesty, being. It's not about product development. How are you going to sell that to publishers, patrons and audience? Let them get their own. It is a rigorous individuality she holds out, living alone at 94, spreading her past and future out upon the dryer to see what else she can do without. In the end it is pure survival.

Daniel restored Nebuchadnezzar's dream. He remembered it for him when he couldn't do it himself, so this "portfolio," paper, paint and ink illustrates her best and worst work, herself. Denial and repression are interesting things. Push it down here, won't it come up there? In the hands of the majority truth can be discounted. But you can't annihilate talent, genius, destiny. It will out like an eclipse where the sun still shines and the effects, if they are known, are even more terrible.

Here on the ground, if a corn of wheat falls and dies, what happens to the gift? It goes down, returns to the soil, recycled like the envelope she keeps her memoir of her mother in, sent originally to

her in 1982 from Bennett Publishing Company with the proof revisions of her sister's book. We wait to learn. Will it show up in the attorney's inventory of the estate? No. She and my old dog are still standing, but not side by side yet. Six mourners at the private gravesite. I guess you're allowed to visit later. Died the same day as the Pope, no other epitaph. Well, one more, buried the same day as the Pope.

Were they able to process her right away or did she have to wait for the crush to die down? After all, it's not every day the Pope arrives and anyway he died first. These and many other questions we wait to answer when satellite communications are restored. Suddenly there is a rash of deaths. Saul Bellow. Prince Rainier, so good conversation anyway. Today the last Pennsylvania Dutchman in our family, Anna Elizabeth Reiff Young, was buried, 1910-2005.

Published September 17, the second day of Rosh Hashanah Year 5784

"Aunt Libby reads as something very personal and precious to you. I love the stories of you on the phone with her. These really help me remember her too. I remember you talking to her, not a specific time, but multiple times, with the beige phone pulled off the stand, sitting on the table, with your notebook out. Perhaps your feet were propped up on the stool. You always listened hard when talking to her. These little memories of my childhood come back slowly. Thank you!" Aeyrie May 16, 2011 at 12:56 PM

Made in the USA
Middletown, DE
01 February 2024

48931243R00136